Living Faiths

T0346862

Buddhism

Mark Constance

Series Editor: Janet Dyson **Consultant:** Robert Bowie

OXFORD
UNIVERSITY PRESS

OXFORD
UNIVERSITY PRESS

Great Clarendon Street, Oxford, OX2 6DP, United Kingdom

Oxford University Press is a department of the University of Oxford. It furthers the University's objective of excellence in research, scholarship, and education by publishing worldwide. Oxford is a registered trade mark of Oxford University Press in the UK and in certain other countries

British Library Cataloguing in Publication Data
Data available

ISBN: 978-0-19-914863-9

11

Paper used in the production of this book is a natural, recyclable product made from wood grown in sustainable forests.
The manufacturing process conforms to the environmental regulations of the country of origin.

Printed in Great Britain by CPI Group (UK) Ltd., Croydon CR0 4YY

Acknowledgements

The publishers would like to thank the following for permissions to use their photographs:

Acknowledgements
The publishers would like to thank the following for permissions to use their photographs:

Cover: Corbis; **p8:** Narathorn/Shutterstock; **p9:** The Art Archive/Alamy; **p12:** Art Directors & TRIP/Alamy; **p15:** AA World Travel Library/Alamy; **p16t:** Gl0ck/Shutterstock; **p16m:** doraclub/Shutterstock; **p16b:** Robert Harding Picture Library Ltd/Alamy; **p17:** defpicture/Shutterstock; **p18:** Cultura Creative/Alamy; **p23:** dbimages/Alamy; **p28:** Horizons WWP/Alamy; **p30:** Calvin Chan/Shutterstock; **p32:** Nadina/Shutterstock; **p33:** The Art Archive/Alamy; **p34:** Kevin Foy/Alamy; **p35:** Karen Hemingway; **p36l:** MS Bretherton/Alamy; **p38t:** Friedrich Stark/Alamy; **p38bl:** Krzysztof Kostrubiec/Shutterstock; **p38br:** Patcharin Yimpatna and the Dhammakaya Temple, UK; **p39:** Santibhavank P/Shutterstock.com; **p41l:** Phaitoon Sutunyawatchai/Shutterstock; **p41r:** dbimages/Alamy; **p42t:** Nick Cornish/Rex Features; **p44t:** Art Directors & TRIP/Alamy; **p44b:** AFP/Getty Images; **p46t:** Mary Kate Denny/Getty Images; **p46bl:** Ursula Gahwiler/Robert Harding/Rex Features; **p46br:** National Geographic/Getty Images; **p47:** Valeria73/Shutterstock; **p49:** AFP/Getty Images; **p52:** Sipa Press/Rex Features; **p53l:** Hemis/Alamy; **p53r:** Getty Images; **p54l:** ZUMA Press, Inc./Alamy; **p54r:** AFP/Getty Images; **p55l:** NIVIERE/SIPA/Rex Features; **p55r:** AFP/Getty Images; **p56l:** Getty Images; **p56r:** AlamyCelebrity/Alamy; **p57:** David Levenson/Alamy; **p58:** TOBY MELVILLE/Reuters/Corbis; **p60:** CBW/Alamy; **p61t:** EQUINOX GRAPHICS/SCIENCE PHOTO LIBRARY; **p61b:** NASA/JPL-Caltech/DSS; **p64:** Hindustan Times via Getty Images; **p65:** Patcharin Yimpatna and the Dhammakaya Temple, UK; **p66:** Pep Roig/Alamy; **p67t:** Paul Springett 10/Alamy; **p67b:** Annabelle Breakey/Getty Images; **p68:** s_bukley/Shutterstock.com; **p71t:** silvergull/Shutterstock; **p71b:** anyaivanova/Shutterstock; **p73t:** Imaginechina/Corbis; **p73b:** donsimon/Shutterstock; **p74:** AFP/Getty Images; **p75l:** Matthew Chattle/Alamy; **p75r:** ZUMA Wire Service/Alamy; all other photos by OUP

Illustrations: Gareth Clarke

From the author, Mark Constance: I would like to thank the students of Balcarras School who, with their questions, answers, humour and thoughtfulness, have made teaching RE the best job in the school.

OUP wishes to thank the Aldam and Harvey families, as well as the community of the temple Wat Santiwongsaram and Phra Aod Boonyoung in particular, for agreeing to take part in the case study films and to be photographed for this title. We would also like to thank The Buddhist Society, and particularly President Dr Desmond Biddulph, for reviewing this book.

We have consulted with the Pali Text Society in the preparation of this book. For further information on the books of the Pali Canon, see www.palitext.com.

Contents

Introduction

What's it like to be a Buddhist?

The *Living Faiths* series helps you to learn about religion by meeting some young people and their families in the UK. Through the case studies in this book you will find out first-hand how their faith affects the way they live and the moral and ethical decisions they make. The big question you will explore is: What does it *mean* to be a Buddhist in twenty-first century Britain?

The icons indicate where you can actually hear and see young people sharing aspects of their daily lives through film, audio and music. This will help you to reflect on your own experiences, whether you belong to a religion or have a secular view of the world.

Key to icons

Image gallery   Audio   Film   Worksheet   Interactive Activity

The Student Book features

Starter activities get you thinking as soon as your lesson starts!

Activities are colour coded to identify three ways of exploring the rich diversity found within and between faiths. Through the questions and activities you will learn to:

- **think like a theologian**: these questions focus on understanding the nature of religious belief, its symbolism and spiritual significance
- **think like a philosopher**: these questions focus on analysing and debating ideas
- **think like a social scientist**: these questions focus on exploring and analysing why people do what they do and how belief affects action

You will be encouraged to think creatively and critically; to empathize, evaluate and respond to the views of others; to give reasons for your opinions and make connections; and draw conclusions.

Useful Words define the key terms, which appear in bold, to help you easily understand definitions. Meanings of words are also defined in the glossary.

Reflection

There will be time for you to reflect on what you've learned about the beliefs and practices of others and how they link to your own views.

Assessment

At the end of each chapter there is a final assessment task which helps you to show what you have learned.

Ways of helping you to assess your learning are part of every chapter:

- unit objectives set out what you will learn
- it's easy to see what standards you are aiming for using the 'I can' level statements
- you're encouraged to discuss and assess your own and each other's work
- you will feel confident in recognizing the next steps and how to improve.

We hope that you will enjoy reading and watching young people share their views, and that you will in turn gain the skills and knowledge to understand people with beliefs both similar to and different from your own.

Janet Dyson
(Series Editor)

Robert Bowie
(Series Consultant)

Meet the Families!

In this book, you will meet some Buddhist families from across the UK. You can read about their thoughts and views on various topics covered in the book, and also watch their full interviews on the *Buddhism Kerboodle*.

The Harvey family

Tom Harvey and his mother live in North Wales. They follow the Theravada tradition of Buddhism. Mrs Harvey is very involved with the local interfaith programme and she actively helps newcomers to the community. Tom enjoys playing computer games with his friends and, when he isn't on his computer, he is often out socializing in town or at parties.

Molly lives very close to her grandmother in North London. They regularly travel a long way to the Buddhist centre where they practise the Mahayana tradition of Buddhism. Molly enjoys playing the guitar and she is thinking of studying English at university.

The Aldam family

Boonyoung

Phra Aod Boonyoung is a monk who lives in a Birmingham Buddhist temple. He is part of a community of British-Thai Buddhist monks who follow the Theravada tradition. Boonyoung stays in the temple to receive guests who come to pay respect to the Buddha, and he also travels around the UK to teach people meditation.

Overview

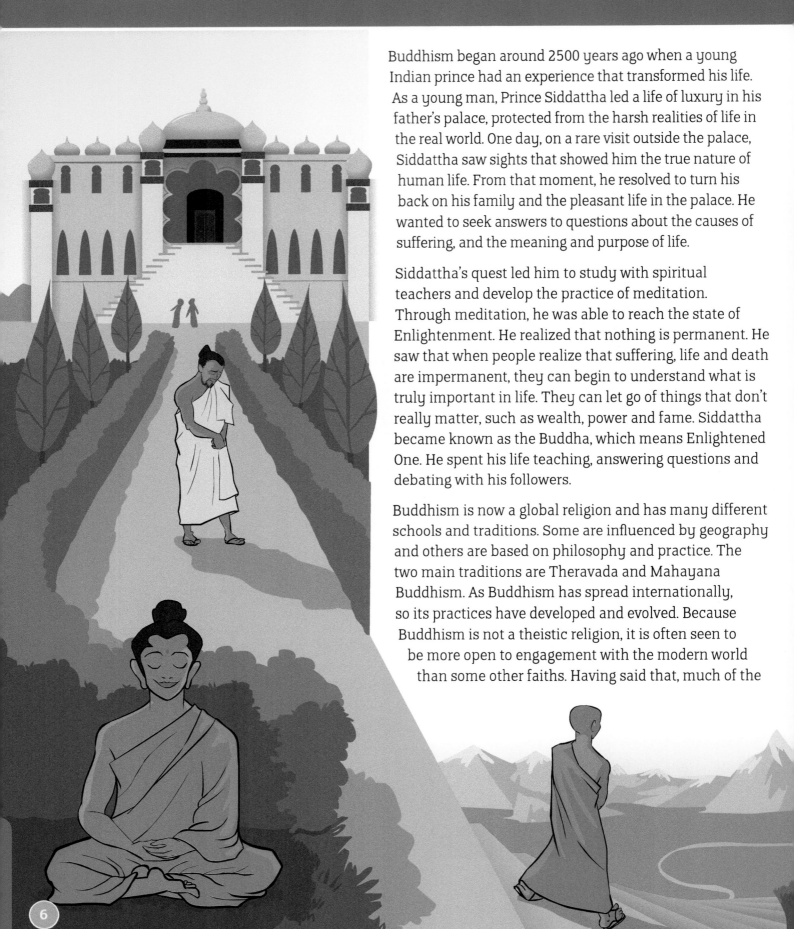

Buddhism began around 2500 years ago when a young Indian prince had an experience that transformed his life. As a young man, Prince Siddattha led a life of luxury in his father's palace, protected from the harsh realities of life in the real world. One day, on a rare visit outside the palace, Siddattha saw sights that showed him the true nature of human life. From that moment, he resolved to turn his back on his family and the pleasant life in the palace. He wanted to seek answers to questions about the causes of suffering, and the meaning and purpose of life.

Siddattha's quest led him to study with spiritual teachers and develop the practice of meditation. Through meditation, he was able to reach the state of Enlightenment. He realized that nothing is permanent. He saw that when people realize that suffering, life and death are impermanent, they can begin to understand what is truly important in life. They can let go of things that don't really matter, such as wealth, power and fame. Siddattha became known as the Buddha, which means Enlightened One. He spent his life teaching, answering questions and debating with his followers.

Buddhism is now a global religion and has many different schools and traditions. Some are influenced by geography and others are based on philosophy and practice. The two main traditions are Theravada and Mahayana Buddhism. As Buddhism has spread internationally, so its practices have developed and evolved. Because Buddhism is not a theistic religion, it is often seen to be more open to engagement with the modern world than some other faiths. Having said that, much of the appeal of Buddhism in a materialistic world lies in its presentation of a simple lifestyle with a focus on living in the moment.

The 2011 Census showed that in Britain, around 248,000 people described themselves as Buddhists, 72% more than in 2001. Many others are interested in the faith, decorating their homes or gardens with images of the Buddha, or attending meditation classes.

Practising Buddhism requires commitment. It involves having a strong ethical code and the discipline to train the mind through meditation. Many Buddhists who want to be ordained as monks or nuns find the training too challenging. To develop the characteristics of patience, wisdom and inner strength takes many years.

Buddhism is unique among world religions because it is not centred around belief in a creator God. Some people feel that as Buddhism has no god, it should be described as a philosophy rather than a religion. At the heart of Buddhism is a desire to understand the world as it really is – something that appeals to many people, whether they are religious or not. Although it is 2500 years since Buddhism began, the teachings of the Buddha continue to interest and engage people all over the world.

What is it about Buddhism that appeals to so many people? As you read this book, you will find that there are many such questions to be explored in order to understand Buddhism as a Living Faith in the twenty-first century.

1.1 Who was the Buddha?

Learning Objectives

In this unit you will:

- investigate who the **Buddha** was
- respond to the story of his early life
- reflect on aspects of your own life.

Starter

- Who is the person in the picture?
- What do you know about him already?

The picture shows an image of the historical Buddha. He is a very important figure in Buddhism and this is his story.

a This statue shows the Buddha in a typical symbolic pose.

The Historical Buddha

The Buddha was an Indian prince called Siddattha Gotama. It is generally accepted that Prince Siddattha was born in Lumbini (in modern Nepal) around 563 **BCE**. When Siddattha was born, some holy men came to visit and said that he would either be a great king or a great holy man. His father hoped he would be a great king, so he gave Siddattha everything he needed within the walls of the palace and sheltered him from any pain, suffering or death.

In Britain, people do not encounter quite as much pain and suffering as some people in other parts of the world. In many ways, we are sheltered from suffering like Siddattha was. Most of us have enough food, comfortable homes, and families to care for us. But Siddattha's father deliberately kept the real world from him. He feared that as soon as his son discovered what the world was really like, he would leave the palace and try to find an answer to the problems of suffering and pain in the world. To keep him in the palace, the king created an alternative reality. Some stories say that Siddattha had a different home to live in within the palace for each season!

In some ways this sounds like a really good life. Sometimes we all want to have everything we wish for, but it was clear that was not enough for Siddattha. He knew that there must be more to life than this. So he asked his friend and charioteer, Channa, to take him outside the palace walls and explain the reality of the world to him, however harsh or unpleasant it was. What do you think happened next?

Useful Words

BCE Stands for 'before the Common Era', which began roughly 2000 years ago

Buddha The Enlightened One; a person who discovers Enlightenment for themself

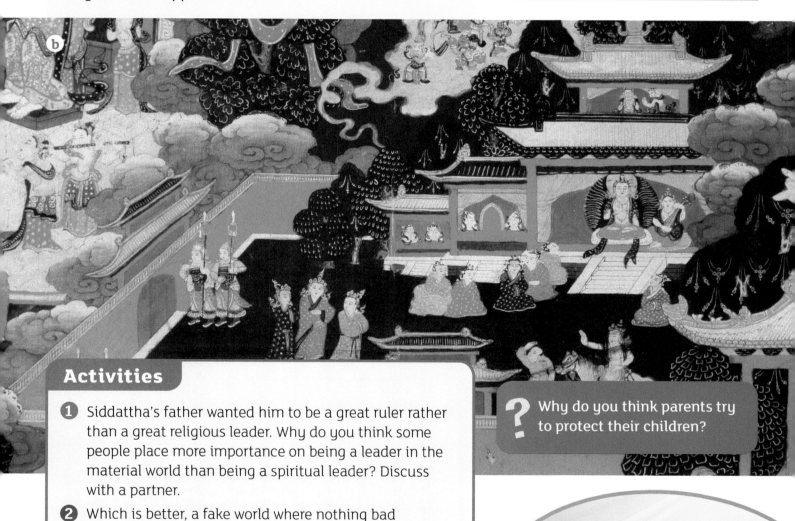

Activities

1. Siddattha's father wanted him to be a great ruler rather than a great religious leader. Why do you think some people place more importance on being a leader in the material world than being a spiritual leader? Discuss with a partner.

2. Which is better, a fake world where nothing bad happens or a real world where there is the possibility of bad things happening? Write a speech explaining your view or a modern story that shows somebody trapped in a fake world.

3. What stories and films, such as *The Matrix*, can you think of that remind you of the story so far? Explain your choice.

? Why do you think parents try to protect their children?

Reflection

Do you think people in Britain live sheltered lives in any way? What things do you think they are sheltered from?

Learning Objectives

In this unit you will:

- understand the impact of the **Four Sights** on Siddattha
- reflect on how human beings are affected by suffering
- reflect on the different types of suffering around you.

Starter

- What sights shock you?
- How do you respond to these things?

The Four Sights

Despite having a beautiful wife and family, excellent job prospects and all the comfort he could want, Prince Siddattha was not satisfied. He decided to go on a journey beyond the palace walls because he was sure there was more to life than what he had already seen (see Unit 1.1).

Siddattha saw four things outside the palace that made a huge impact on him. Buddhists know these as the Four Sights.

The first sight was old age. In the palace, Siddattha was surrounded by things that were beautiful and youthful, so this was the first time that he had seen old age and its effects on a person's body.

The next sight was a sick man. Illness was something else that Siddattha had never known and he was deeply troubled by it.

Next, Siddattha saw a funeral taking place. He had never known death before, so this distressed him even more, since he had to face the finality of death and the suffering it caused those who were left behind.

Siddattha's guide, Channa, explained that all these things happen to everyone eventually.

a Siddattha was shocked by human suffering.

'What is the noble truth of suffering? Birth is suffering; aging is suffering; sickness is suffering, death is suffering; being in contact with what is displeasing is suffering; not to get what one wants is suffering.'
Samyutta Nikāya 56:11

? Make a small mind-map to show what types of suffering there are around you and within your local community.

After seeing the horrifying realities of old age, sickness and death, the final sight gave Siddattha some hope. He saw a **samana**, a holy man who wore simple clothes and carried a begging bowl. What surprised Siddattha was that this man was happy even though he had nothing.

Together, the Four Sights made it clear to Siddattha that his wealth and family could not protect him from the painful realities of life. Since he knew what life was really like, there was no way he could ever return to the security of the palace. He decided that he must dedicate the rest of his life to finding a way to end the suffering in the world.

So Siddattha became a samana and began his spiritual journey.

b The holy man seemed happy in his poverty.

Useful Words

Samana A holy man who lives a life of poverty

Four Sights The four sights that deeply affected Siddattha: an old man, a sick man, a dead body and a holy man

Reflection

Do you think there is a way to end all the suffering in the world?

Activities

1 Why do you think Siddattha could no longer live in the palace? Put yourself in his shoes and write or draw your response as a piece of poetry or art.

2 Read the quotation on the opposite page and share your mind-map with a partner. Explain how each point could be described as suffering.

3 Do you think that becoming a holy man was the right thing for Siddattha to do? Make a list of other ways Siddattha could have responded to suffering and give a reason for each suggestion.

4 'With so much suffering, how can life mean anything?' 'There must be a greater purpose to life.' Imagine a conversation between these two people. What might they say to try and convince one another?

Learning Objectives

In this unit you will:

- explore the meaning of **anicca**, **dukkha** and **anatta**
- explain how the **Three Signs of Being** led to the Buddha's **Enlightenment**
- reflect on the Buddha's teachings about change, suffering and the self.

Enlightenment

After six years, Siddattha realized that being a samana was not going to provide him with a solution to all the suffering in the world. He left the holy men and sat under a **Bodhi tree** to meditate. He had given up everything: his life at the palace and his newfound spiritual life. Neither had revealed the answers he was looking for.

Over the next few nights he found the knowledge he was looking for and saw the world and life as they really are. In this way, he found Enlightenment and became known as the Buddha, the Enlightened One. He began to teach others about what he discovered and how they could be freed from the endless cycle of suffering (see Unit 2.6).

Useful Words

Bodhi tree A type of fig tree
Enlightenment The state of full understanding about the way things are in life
Three Signs of Being Anicca, dukkha, anatta

a There are many artistic representations of the Buddha meditating under the Bodhi tree.

The Buddha taught for about 50 years and his teachings (**dhamma**) can be described in three parts: the Three Signs of Being, the Four Noble Truths (see Unit 1.4) and the Noble Eightfold Path (see Unit 2.3).

The discoveries that the Buddha made during his Enlightenment are called the Three Signs of Being: anicca, dukkha and anatta.

Anicca means that everything changes and nothing lasts forever. The Buddha taught that it is important to understand that everything in the world is temporary, because if people appreciate that nothing is permanent, they will value life much more.

Case Study

> Everything that comes into being also ceases [ends], whatever it is. [...] when a flower blooms, that ceases, but also the solar system will one day cease, so everything is going to cease.

Molly lives near her grandmother, Mrs Aldam, in North London, and they are both Buddhists.

Dukkha is sometimes translated as suffering, but that does not grasp the true meaning. It includes physical suffering and pain, but also suffering of the mind, such as anxiety, stress and general dissatisfaction with life. One way to understand dukkha is to imagine a bicycle with a seriously buckled wheel. If you ride this bicycle, you will always feel that something is not right and could be better.

Buddhists recognize that people have lots of desires, but even when they get what they want, they are often dissatisfied and want the next bigger or better thing. The Buddha taught that all of life is dukkha and that knowing this is essential.

Anatta is the Buddhist belief that there is no permanent self or 'soul'. People often try to hold onto who or what they used to be, but Buddhists believe that people cannot stop changing. As people grow older, their bodies, minds and personalities change. Friendships and families change. The Buddha taught that no aspect of a person is everlasting (lasts forever).

Reflection

Mrs Aldam talks about the idea that everything ends eventually. What do you think she means? Would such a belief help you understand the world?

Activities

1. List seven examples of things in life that Buddhists would call dukkha.

2. Do you think that the Three Signs of Being are an accurate view of how this life and the world are? Can you think of anything in life that does not change? Discuss with a partner.

3. Molly's grandmother says that everything ceases or ends eventually. Draw five things in life that have beginnings and endings (for example, seasons, fashion styles, people).

1.4 Seeking the Truth

Learning Objectives

In this unit you will:

- explore the **Four Noble Truths**
- analyse the causes and effects of **craving** things
- reflect on your own views about wanting things.

Starter

- What single thing would improve your quality of life significantly right now?
- What thing have you wanted most in your life?

Some of the Buddha's earliest teachings were about finding a '**Middle Way**' in life: not living a life of great excess and extravagance on one hand, nor a life of great poverty on the other. These early teachings are called the Four Noble Truths.

One common way of understanding the Four Noble Truths is to imagine the Buddha as a doctor who diagnoses an illness, explains its cause, makes it clear there is a cure, and finally, gives the cure.

Buddhists believe that if these Four Noble Truths are accepted, people can be 'cured' and change the way they see the world.

The Buddha taught that the Four Noble Truths are:

1 Illness
Nothing is perfect and all life involves suffering. It is important to accept that everything in the world is dukkha.

2 Cause
People act selfishly. Whatever they have is not enough and they always want more. This craving causes dukkha.

3 Cure exists
If people are satisfied, understand reality, and stop craving things, dukkha will end. This is not easy, but it is possible.

4 Cure
The way to stop craving is to take the Middle Way, by following the Buddha's teachings in the Noble Eightfold Path (see Unit 2.3).

> '*I teach suffering, its origin, cessation and path.*'
> The Buddha, *Majjhima Nikāya 63*

> '*Craving fuels suffering in the way that wood fuels a fire ...*'
> Damien Keown in *Buddhism: A Very Short Introduction*

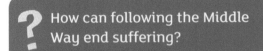

? How can following the Middle Way end suffering?

a

Useful Words

Craving A constant desire for things and experiences

Case Study

Molly says, 'Being a Buddhist means I am not so influenced by others who want these [consumer] products and fashions, although I do have a smartphone, but that was a gift from a friend and I hope I wouldn't mind if I lost it. I know that getting what I want won't actually give me the satisfaction I think it will. If I get something that I really desire, eventually the pleasure will fade and it will be boring and I will start to want something else, or I will lose it and then I will start asking for something else. So, I will not put so much emphasis on material possessions.'

b

? How would you feel if you could not go shopping any more?

Reflection

If you had fewer things, do you think you would have a better life?

Activities

1. What do you think the underlying causes of our greed and selfishness are? With a partner, make a list of what you think they are.

2. Do you think that an absence of craving, greed and selfishness would make you a happier person? Prepare two short speeches, one arguing that this would make you happier and the other arguing that it would not.

3. Why do you think that the Buddha saw a link between selfishness and suffering? Note down three examples of links between selfishness and suffering.

4. For the Buddha, true happiness comes from letting go of things. Why do you think people today find this difficult? Create a storyboard about someone who finds true happiness by letting go of something that everyone else thinks is important.

1.5 Symbols: Making Meaning

Learning Objectives

In this unit you will:

- identify what symbols mean and why they are important
- explain some important symbols for Buddhists
- reflect on the significance of symbols in everyday life.

Starter

- Are you wearing any symbols or can you see any around you?
- What do you think makes a symbol effective?

A symbol is an image that points towards something deeper and more significant. Symbols are all around us – for example, on clothes and packaged food. Companies pay a lot of money for someone to design a logo that says something about who they are and what they stand for in a simple, eye-catching way.

Buddhists use many symbols. Three of the most famous are images of the Buddha, the **Dhamma Wheel** and the **lotus flower**.

Images of the Buddha take many different forms. Because anyone has the potential to be a Buddha and become Enlightened, images do not always take the form of the historical Buddha. It is becoming more common in Western societies to have images of Buddhas.

Traditional images of the historical Buddha often have distinctive symbolic features. The Buddha is often shown in one of three positions: standing, sitting or lying down. When standing, the Buddha usually has one hand raised as a sign of blessing. The Buddha meditates sitting down with his legs crossed in the lotus position. His right hand can be in various positions, each with a different meaning. For example, his right hand touching the earth symbolizes the Buddha telling the earth to pay attention to his teachings. An image of the Buddha lying down symbolizes the end of his life, when his worldly suffering came to an end.

? What does this logo mean to you?

a

b The Dhamma Wheel is a symbolic respresentation of the Buddha's teachings on the way to Enlightenment.

c In many images of the Buddha he is shown with curly hair, a bump on his head called an ushnisha, a third eye and long, dangly earlobes. Find out what these things symbolize.

The wheel is one of the oldest symbols in Buddhism and is often used to represent the dhamma. The Dhamma Wheel, or **Dhammacakka**, has many meanings within it. The eight spokes represent the Noble Eightfold Path (see Unit 2.3). The hub of the wheel represents discipline, which is essential to Buddhist life. The circle of the wheel shows that the dhamma (teaching of the Buddha) is perfect and complete.

The lotus flower is similar to a water lily. It rises to the surface from the mud at the bottom of a pond. The mud does not make the flower dirty – it looks beautiful in full bloom above the water. This symbolizes the way the Buddha taught that people can rise above the unsatisfactory things and sufferings in life and achieve Enlightenment. The Buddha is sometimes shown meditating on a lotus flower.

d This traditional Chinese wall painting shows both the lotus flower and a symbolic pose.

Useful Words

Dhamma Wheel (Dhammacakka)
A wheel with eight spokes that is a symbol of Buddhism and respresents the Noble Eightfold Path
Lotus flower A flower that is similar to a water lily and is a symbol of Buddhism

Reflection

Why do you think that many brands, schools and companies care so much about the symbols they use?

Activities

1 Which of the symbols mentioned do you think best symbolizes Buddhism? Compare your answer with a partner.

2 Design your own symbol to communicate one of the key teachings of Buddhism that you have looked at so far. You can borrow some ideas from the images in this unit. Do not include words, so the symbol can be used by any Buddhist no matter what language they speak.

3 Choose one of the images of the Buddha or symbols that appeals to you. Sit quietly, looking carefully at the image. Note down your feelings about it.

4 Interview your head teacher or a senior member of staff about the school badge or logo and what it means.

Learning Objectives

In this unit you will:

- examine Buddhist beliefs on life, death and rebirth
- explain the meaning and importance of **kamma**
- reflect on the effects of your actions on yourself and others.

Starter

- How do you want to be remembered when you die?
- Have you ever had the feeling that you have lived before?

In Britain today, death is something people do not like to think or talk about. Although everyone has to die one day, many people have a great fear of death.

Buddhists recognize that death is inevitable, as everything is impermanent. However, it is this **impermanence** that makes life special, unique and beautiful. If you compare your thumbprint with a partner's, you will see they are different. No one, anywhere, has the same thumbprint as you.

Tibetan Buddhists (see Unit 4.2) believe that meditating on death is very important. Some Buddhists even visit cemeteries to prepare themselves for the inevitability of death. Buddhists believe that when people die, wealth, social standing, jobs and possessions do not matter. What does matter is how you have lived, and this has an effect on what happens when you die. Buddhists believe that after they die all living things are reborn according to their kamma.

Case Study

Mrs Aldam says 'all my actions have consequences'. She thinks that what we do in our present lives will affect our future lives and explains how 'this has made me treat people differently and I do not feel hatred for anyone'. Mrs Aldam feels that this has helped her make sense of why some people seem to have so much and other people suffer so much.

a Like thumbprints, we are all unique.

Useful Words

Impermanence When something doesn't last and can change
Kamma/karma Actions that are the result of the choices people make
Samsara The endless cycle of birth, death and rebirth, with all its suffering

'It is choice [...] that I call kamma.'
The Buddha, *Anguttara Nikāya*

Case Study

Mrs Harvey also believes that all our actions have very real consequences. She says that if she kills anything, it will have a consequence for her: 'If I am watering the plants and there are loads of ants in there, I have to avoid [them] because I know that I am going to flood them. If I flood those ants, later on I will be flooded.'

Mrs Harvey is also a Buddhist. She lives in Wales with her son, Tom.

Kamma, or karma, means action. It refers to the actions that are the result of the choices people make. Buddhists believe that if a person chooses to do bad things, they will suffer the consequences. If a person chooses to do good things, there will be good consequences. Everyone carries around both the positive and negative consequences of their actions. But kamma is not a system of rewards and punishments. It is something that people bring about themselves.

Buddhists believe that the kamma a person builds up in this life will determine the nature of their rebirth, which is part of the endless cycle of birth, death and rebirth called **samsara** (see Unit 2.6). The only way to escape from this cycle is to follow the Buddha's teachings and seek Enlightenment.

b Good deeds build positive kamma.

Reflection

If you believed in kamma, do you think that it would make you behave, act and live differently to the way you do now?

Activities

1. Write an email to tell a friend how you would like to be remembered, and about the memorable things you have done in your life.

2. 'Death is not the end.' Write down your own response as well as a response from someone who holds different beliefs. How would a Buddhist respond?

3. Note down three examples from your life where you can see the consequences of your actions on yourself and other people.

4. Prepare questions to hot-seat Mrs Aldam and Mrs Harvey, asking them to explain their beliefs about kamma.

Chapter 1 Assessment
What do Buddhists Believe?

Objectives

- Examine the Four Noble Truths and the effect they have on Buddhists' lives.
- Interpret the teachings of the Buddha for modern life.
- Reflect on your own ideas about whether there is a cure for the suffering in the world.

Task

Design and make a poster for a doctor's surgery waiting room. On the poster, explain the symptoms of the 'illness' the Buddha said people are suffering from, and what the cure is. Include specific religious terms, but also be clear and straightforward so that it can be understood by everyone. You could include some Buddhist symbols or images to show that the poster is based on Buddhist teachings. You could also include some quotations from this chapter. Make a note of your thoughts so you can share them in a class discussion.

A bit of guidance...

Aim to explain and present these important teachings in a clear, relevant and thought-provoking way. If there is any information that does not fit on the poster, you could also produce a small leaflet to accompany it.

Hints and tips

To help you tackle this task, you could:

- give examples of the symptoms the Buddha talked about, drawing inspiration from the things around you, and your life and experience
- use the case studies in this chapter to show how these teachings have already affected some people's lives.

Guidance

What level are you aiming at? Have a look at the grid opposite to see what you need to do to achieve that level. What would you need to do to improve your work?

	I can...
Level 3	• use some religious terms to give a brief description of the Four Noble Truths and make links between this and how Buddhists live • begin to identify the impact of Buddhism on people's lives and the relevance of its teachings today • express my ideas about ways of dealing with suffering linked to my learning about Buddhism.
Level 4	• use a range of religious terms to show a clear understanding of the Four Noble Truths and the impact they have on the lives of people who follow the teachings of the Buddha • respond by using clear examples about suffering in the world and suggest some answers to suffering • express my ideas about ways of dealing with suffering in the world in the light of my learning about Buddhist teachings.
Level 5	• describe the impact of the Four Noble Truths, showing that I understand a good range of religious vocabulary • give reasons and examples as to why these beliefs are important to Buddhists • express a well-informed opinion about the nature and causes of suffering, and ways of responding to it, drawing on Buddhist teaching.
Level 6	• interpret the significance and impact of the Four Noble Truths, showing a well-developed understanding of a wide range of religious vocabulary • analyse the case studies and apply the beliefs expressed, presenting them in a clear and coherent manner • evaluate my own and others' perspectives on the nature and causes of suffering and solutions to it in the light of my understanding of Buddhist teaching.

Ready for more?

When you have completed this task, you can also work on your skills for Levels 6 and 7, and perhaps even higher. **This is an extension task.**

'Beliefs affect actions.' Do you agree with this statement? Do some research on this idea from the points of view of Buddhism and one other faith you have studied. Then write an essay based on the statement. You can compare and contrast how beliefs affect actions within the two faiths as well as explaining how your beliefs and values affect the way you live.

Learning Objectives

In this unit you will:

- evaluate the importance of scripture to religious believers
- explain how and why Buddhists use key scriptures
- reflect on the nature of religious wisdom and life experience.

Starter

- What are the sources of authority in your life?
- In the game Chinese Whispers, a message is whispered from person to person. By the end, the message has usually changed. Why?

What do you think about when you hear the word 'authority'? Maybe a judge or a courtroom comes to mind. Perhaps your parents, teachers or the police. For many religious believers, authority is found in the scriptures of their religion. They provide a source of inspiration, faith and guidance on the correct path.

The Buddha lived at a time when most people memorized all the details of stories, songs and teachings. The Buddha's teachings were passed down by word of mouth in this way for hundreds of years before anybody wrote them down.

When they were first gathered together, the teachings were written in **Pali**. A later collection of writings was also put together in the **Sanskrit** language. This is why there are sometimes two slightly different words for important Buddhist ideas, such as kamma or karma. One word is from the Pali **Canon** and the other is from the Sanskrit Canon, which are both collections of Buddhist writings.

*'Although reciting a large number of scriptual texts, if being careless he does not act accordingly [...] he has no share in the **ascetic's** life.'*
The Buddha, *Dhammapada 19*

? What do you think the Buddha meant by this?

a The teachings of the Buddha exist in both the Pali and Sanskrit languages.

The Pali Canon is also known as the **Tipitaka**, which means 'The Three Baskets'. It is thought that this name comes from when the teachings were written on long, narrow leaves, bound together and stored in baskets.

These teachings are very important for many Buddhists and fall into three categories.

- The **Vinaya basket** contains hundreds of guidelines that Buddhist monks and nuns have to follow.

- The **Sutta basket** contains the most well-known teachings and sayings of the Buddha. It is divided into five nikayas, or collections.

- The **Abhidhamma** (which means 'higher teaching') **basket** contains discussions on how to understand and interpret the Buddha's teachings.

Some Buddhists also follow the teachings in the Sanskrit Canon. Although these were written down later than the Pali Canon, many Buddhists consider them to be genuine teachings of the Buddha. Two of the most important scriptures of the Sanskrit Canon are the Heart Sutra and the Diamond Sutra.

Scriptures provide Buddhists with clear teachings and a framework to live by. That is why they are often kept in a special place in a monastery, temple or home. But it should be remembered that how a Buddhist lives is also very important. Some Buddhists place more importance on the individual's experience than on the scriptures – they think that life experiences and the teachings of their spiritual teachers are the best guides to live by.

Useful Words

Ascetic Someone who lives a life of self-denial, often in order to reach a spiritual goal
Canon A collection of sacred writings
Pali The language of many early Buddhist scriptures; an ancient language originating in northern India
Sanskrit The ancient sacred language of India
Sutta/sutra Text; the word of the Buddha

b Scripture provides Buddhists with guidelines for life.

Reflection

Which do you think people can learn more from: scripture or their life experiences?

Activities

1 It is clear that scriptures are important for Buddhists. Why do you think that people find guidelines for life useful?

2 Make a decorated bookmark to give to a young child. It should explain why scriptures are important to Buddhists and how they are used.

3 In groups, write notes for a discussion between a politician, a care worker and a successful pop singer on their guidelines for living.

4 Choose a song or story that you find inspiring and note down how it makes you feel.

2.2 How can Stories Inspire?

Learning Objectives

In this unit you will:

- explain the importance of the Jataka Tales for Buddhists
- reflect on the meaning behind a story.

Starter

- What childhood stories do you remember best and why?
- Why are stories a good way of teaching about moral choices?

Many people remember stories they were told when they were young. Good stories are often timeless and frequently have a deeper meaning.

The Jataka Tales, originally from the Sutta basket of the Pali Canon (see Unit 2.1), are stories about the previous lives of the Buddha, where he appears both in animal and human form. The tales give people a clearer understanding of the world and of the right way to live their lives. Each story teaches a moral message through the experience of particular characters. One of the stories is about the Monkey King.

The Monkey King and the Mangoes

There once was a band of monkeys that lived in a huge mango tree next to a river. The monkeys had a very good life, with lots of delicious mangoes to eat. The Monkey King told them not to let any mangoes fall into the river because they would travel downstream to the city and the humans would want to eat them.

One day, one of the mangoes dropped into the river and travelled to the city. The human king tasted the mango and loved it. He realized it must have come from a tree upstream. So he ordered his soldiers to sail up the river to look for the tree.

The monkeys saw the humans coming and hid in the tree. But the human king saw one of the monkeys' tails peeking out between the leaves. He was furious and worried that they would eat what he now considered to be *his* fruit from *his* tree. He ordered his soldiers to light a fire so that he could have roast monkey with the delicious mangoes.

a The tale of the Monkey King defines what makes a good leader.

The Monkey King had an idea. He ran along a branch hanging over the river and leapt to the other side. He tied a long piece of twine around his waist and jumped back to the tree. But the twine was too short so the Monkey King had to cling to the branch, suspended in mid-air. He told the monkeys to use his body as a bridge and cross to safety on the other side of the river. They all crossed the river, but as the last one crossed, the Monkey King was unable to move. His back was broken.

One of the soldiers aimed an arrow to shoot the Monkey King. But the human king stopped him because he had seen the Monkey King's amazing sacrifice. They took the Monkey King down and asked why he had risked his own life to save the others. He answered, 'My monkeys are safe now. That is all that matters. If you want to be a good king, you must resolve to help other people.' With these final words, he died.

The human king knew the Monkey King had taught him what it really meant to be a king. He gave the Monkey King a very respectful burial and built a huge monument as a symbol of his courage and sacrifice.

Activities

1 List three questions you would like to ask in order to explore the deeper meaning of the story. Discuss your questions with a partner.

2 Research some of the other Jataka Tales from the Pali Canon. Choose one and make a cartoon that tells the story in a clear way for young children. Include speech and captions.

Reflection

How do you think that you could use one of the Jataka Tales to develop your character?

3 Write a decorated inscription for a monument to commemorate the Monkey King's achievements.

Learning Objectives

In this unit you will:

- analyse the Buddha's teaching on finding the right way
- find out about how Buddhists try to shape their lives according to the Buddha's teachings
- reflect on the idea of a world without suffering.

Starter

- How do you know whether something is right or wrong?

In life, we are presented with so many different paths to follow that it can sometimes be bewildering. Your teachers probably have one set of ideas about the choices you should make, including getting your homework in on time! Your parents will have other ideas, and yours may be completely different.

The Buddha experienced a life of complete luxury and also a life of complete poverty and self-denial. Neither provided him with the answers he was looking for. Instead, he found Enlightenment by following what he called the Middle Way. It is the path between the extremes of excess on the one hand, and hardship on the other. The Buddha said that the Middle Way is like playing a stringed instrument – if you pull them too tight, the strings will break, but if they're too loose, you get no sound. According to the Buddha, only the Middle Way can lead to **Nibbana** (or Nirvana).

a The Middle Way means avoiding extremes of excess and hardship in life.

'Nibbana' means 'blown out', rather like a candle being blown out. Buddhists believe that Nibbana is the state of perfect peace that comes from 'blowing out' the 'fires' of greed, hatred and ignorance. It is freedom from the endless cycle of birth, death and rebirth (see Unit 2.6).

The Buddha's teaching about the Middle Way is outlined in the **Noble Eightfold Path**. This is a guide for living in the right way with the right attitudes.

b A stringed instrument with strings too loose and too tight is a good way to remember what the Middle Way means.

The eight points of the Noble Eightfold Path work together. It advises how to treat others, how to think about yourself and how to see the world. It is also advises on the right things to say and spend time on.

Reflection
What would a world without suffering be like?

8 Right Contemplation
Concentrate the mind, get rid of bad thoughts and find mental calm.

1 Right Understanding
See the world as it is, accept the existence of Dukkha and understand there is a path to freedom.

7 Right Mindfulness
Be constantly aware of thoughts and actions, and their possible consequences.

2 Right Attitude
Make a serious commitment to develop the right mental attitude and thoughts.

6 Right Effort
Work hard to make all thought, speech and actions positive.

3 Right Speech
Speak in a positive, truthful and helpful way.

5 Right Livelihood
Earn a living in an honest way that does not harm any living thing.

4 Right Action
Be honest, content and faithful. Do not kill any living thing or use harmful substances.

c The Noble Eightfold Path is often represented by a wheel with eight spokes.

Useful Words

Nibbana/Nirvana 'Blowing out' the fires of greed, hatred and ignorance, and the state of perfect peace that follows
Noble Eightfold Path The Buddha's Middle Way

Activities

1. You are a member of the school council. How might you use the Noble Eightfold Path to help you draw up guidelines for living in the school community?

2. Imagine a Buddhist whose approach to their job is inspired by the Noble Eightfold Path. Describe in detail how the Path might affect how they do their job.

3. What kind of jobs do you think Buddhists would not do? Make a list and explain your reasons for including each job.

Case Study

Molly says, 'ultimately the Noble Eightfold Path leads to Enlightenment, which leads to freedom from suffering, but I think generally it leads to a more beneficial and happier life if you follow it. Right Speech includes avoiding pointless babble and gossip, and I find that really hard to avoid, especially at school. [...] But also, I find mindfulness and concentration really hard because I can't focus on one thing for too long.'

2.4 The Five Precepts

Learning Objectives

In this unit you will:

- identify the features of the Five Precepts
- identify ways of following Buddhist guidelines in everyday life
- reflect on how easy it is to change actions and behaviour.

Starter

- What qualities in yourself do you like? Which would you like to develop?

Everyone lives by moral and **ethical** codes. Buddhists are no exception, but they do not have a strict set of rules or laws, since choices can be right or wrong in different situations. **Lay** Buddhists (those who are not monks or nuns) try to live by the **Five Precepts**. These form a practical and ethical guide to how people should conduct themselves based on common sense.

Useful Words

Ethical Living and working by doing the 'right' thing
Five Precepts Practical ethical guidelines for living a Buddhist life
Lay People who follow a faith but are not ordained

Case Study

Tom Harvey grew up in a Buddhist family. The Five Precepts have always been a big part of his life because his mum taught him that they were important. He says, 'I just follow them naturally and don't have to give them too much thought. They are part of who I am.'

a Unlike lay Buddhists, monks and nuns have clear guidelines by which they must live.

All the Five Precepts start with 'I will avoid...'. Negative actions should be avoided and positive actions encouraged. The Buddhist concept of kamma (see Unit 1.6) means that actions have consequences. So positive actions and behaviours give positive results.

The Five Precepts are very practical and define the way Buddhists live. Many Buddhists are vegetarian and many believe it is important to care for the natural world (First Precept). Buddhists also believe that human relationships are very important. They think that people should respect each other and that sex is intended to be part of a loving and committed relationship (Third Precept), for example.

Buddhists value honesty and generosity, as shown in the Second and Fourth Precepts. Buddhism is also concerned with 'seeing' things the right way. It is only when people are truly aware of the world around them and how things are that they start to see things clearly. This cannot happen if they are drunk or under the influence of drugs (Fifth Precept).

? For each of the negative actions to avoid, suggest what you think is the positive opposite.

b

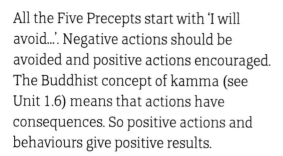

The Five Precepts

1. I will avoid taking life.

2. I will avoid taking what is not given.

3. I will avoid harmful sexual activity.

4. I will avoid saying what is not true.

5. I will avoid drinking alcohol and taking harmful drugs.

Reflection

Is it possible to change how you act and behave?

Activities

1. Although the Five Precepts are all important to Buddhists, rank them in the order of importance to yourself. Give your reasons.

2. Create a role-play that explores the challenges of following one of the Precepts.

3. Write a story or create a comic strip about a modern Buddhist who lives their life by the Five Precepts. Think about the challenges that life would offer, and how they would overcome negative actions and develop positive actions. Consider both a school and a home life example.

4. Tom says that he grew up following the Five Precepts. Make a list of five guidelines that are important to you. Be prepared to present them to the class.

Learning Objectives

In this unit you will:

- investigate a special day for Buddhists
- identify the main features of the Buddhist festival of Wesak
- reflect on your own ideas about religious celebrations.

Starter

- What's the best party you have ever been to? Why?
- Do you celebrate any religious events?

Most people take any excuse for a party. They love to celebrate special events and occasions, and mark them in different ways. Buddhism also has its own festivals, and while Buddhists in different areas of the world might have their own set of traditions, one festival that Buddhists all over the world celebrate is **Wesak**.

Wesak is held on the day of the full moon in the month of Wesak, which is in May or June in Britain. It is a festival to remember three very important events in the Buddha's life: his birth, Enlightenment and death. Some Buddhists believe that all three events happened on the same day.

At Wesak, people often visit temples and monasteries. These temples are beautifully decorated and people show their respect to the Buddha by pouring scented water over the **Buddharupa** (image of the Buddha). People give each other cards and presents. Monks give special talks to lay Buddhists on the life and teachings of the Buddha. At night, the Buddharupa is taken out of the temple and people light candles or carry lanterns around it. This surrounds the Buddha in light to represent how he taught people how to become Enlightened.

a Wesak processions, like this one in Kuala Lumpur, Malaysia, often feature many bright lights and candles.

Case Study

At Wesak, Tom Harvey and his mother visit a Buddhist temple. They give gifts to the monks and help to serve food that they have brought. Later in the day, they take part in a candle celebration surrounding the image of the Buddha with light. This is a special day for them because they can show their respect for the Buddha and also have a great time with their friends.

Useful Words

Buddharupa An image of the Buddha
Wesak A festival on the full moon in the month of Wesak (in May or June) to celebrate the birth, Enlightenment and death of the Buddha

Reflection

'Life would be dull without celebrations.' Do you agree?

Activities

① What questions would you like to ask the Harvey family about how and why they celebrate Wesak?

② Compare what your have learned about Wesak with what you know about other religious festivals such as Eid, Christmas and Divali. What do they have in common? Which parts of the festival are religious and which are mainly social?

③ 'People with no religion should not celebrate religious festivals.' Do you agree with this statement? Write an answer explaining clearly what you think. Remember to show that you understand why some people might have views that are different from your own.

④ You have been asked by a group of Buddhists in Thailand to plan their Wesak celebrations this year. Design a card, give some gift suggestions and plan a special meal for the day. Also plan what will happen when the Buddharupa is taken out of the temple and surrounded by light. Put together an event plan for them.

2.6 Life and Death: the Never-Ending Circle

Learning Objectives

In this unit you will:

- examine Buddhist beliefs on life and death
- explore the concepts of samsara and Nibbana
- reflect on the impermanence of life.

Starter

- Do you think that life has a definite end?
- What do you think happens when you die?

This wheel is a **Bhavacakka** or Wheel of Life. It shows six realms that people can inhabit.

Buddhists believe that life is an endless cycle of birth, death and rebirth called **samsara**. At the end of a life, a person is reborn into one of the six realms. The number of times a person can be reborn is endless. Where they go depends on the moral choices they have made and the kamma that they built up (see Unit 1.6).

Some realms look more pleasant than others. Some are heavenly realms and others are like versions of hell. But it is important to realize that, for Buddhists, all these states are dukkha. They all feature suffering and are unsatisfactory.

Buddhists strive to find freedom from suffering and samsara, and reach the state of perfect peace called Nibbana (see Unit 2.3). They can only do this by fulfilling their potential for goodness and wisdom, and reaching Enlightenment.

? What can you see in this picture?

32

The Buddha reached Enlightenment during his lifetime. Buddhists believe that he could have passed into Nibbana immediately, but instead he chose to stay and spent the rest of his life travelling, teaching and helping others. He died when he was about 80 years old. Buddhists celebrate his death on **Nibbana Day** in February when they believe the Buddha reached his final Nibbana.

On Nibbana Day, Buddhists often meet socially at monasteries to eat together and give gifts. They take the opportunity to think about their own lives and spend much of the day meditating. They think about how they can work towards an end to suffering and strive towards Nibbana. They also reflect on the impermanence of life, and think about loved ones who have died.

There will often be readings of some of the last teachings of the Buddha.

b Pure Land Buddhists (see Unit 3.4) believe that by meditating on Amida Buddha, they can be reborn into a 'pure land', which is closer to a final Nibbana.

'This process of repeated rebirth is known as samsara, […] a term suggesting continuous movement like the flow of a river.'
Damien Keown, *Buddhism: A Very Short Introduction*

Useful Words

Bhavacakka Buddhist art that represents the universe symbolically
Samsara The endless cycle of birth, death and rebirth, with all its suffering

'All […] things are of a nature to decay – strive on [for Nibbana] untiringly.'
Digha Nikāya

Reflection

What life experiences make the physical world appealing? What might make Nibbana appealing?

Activities

1 Referring to the Bhavacakka opposite, design your own 'wheel' to show your symbolic representation of the universe. You can use people and animals to represent different things. Add a key to explain your design.

2 Write a mini biography celebrating the life of the Buddha.

3 Look carefully at the six realms of existence on a version of the Bhavacakka. What do they show? What links can you make with beliefs about life after death in other faiths you have studied? Make a table showing the similarities and differences.

Learning Objectives

In this unit you will:

- identify what worship means
- investigate different types of Buddhist worship
- reflect on the idea of worship without a god.

Starter

- How do you show respect to someone who is important to you?
- If you wanted to give that person a gift, what would you give them?

Worship simply means showing respect to something or someone. Buddhists do not believe in a god, so the concept of worship might seem slightly strange to some people.

Buddhist worship takes many forms. Some acts of Buddhist worship take place at a shrine and include chanting, making offerings of things such as flowers, water and food, and listening to the scriptures being read. Practices such as martial arts, tea-making and the making of mandalas (see Unit 3.5) can also be seen as acts of worship. Meditation is also very important. There are many strands of Buddhism (see Unit 3.2), so Buddhists worship in many different ways.

Case Study

The monk Boonyoung says that when he worships, he pays respect to the Buddha, because the Buddha is the founder of the dhamma. He says that 'dhamma are the rules to guide us to walk along the [right] path.' He thinks that it is very important to worship with the **Sangha**, the community of Buddhist believers, and that is why he joins with others to pray.

a Buddhists showing respect to a giant Buddha statue in Thailand.

Useful Words

Anjali mudda The gesture of putting the hands together in a prayer-like position and bowing the head

Mantra Words to meditate on and focus the mind

Prostration A movement where the body is laid flat on the ground, with the face down, before getting up again

Puja Buddhist worship

Sangha The community of Buddhist believers

There is no set day of worship for Buddhists and many perform **puja** at home where they may have their own personal shrine. The shrine room in a temple contains a Buddharupa. Buddhists remove their shoes before an act of worship and often sit in the lotus position. Sometimes they bow their heads towards the Buddharupa as a sign of respect, with their hands held together in a traditional prayer-like position. This is called **anjali mudda** in Sanskrit, and is also used by Hindus.

Reflection

Can you be spiritual without being religious?

b Mrs Aldam worships in private at her home shrine

Case Study

Mrs Aldam has a little shrine at home. She says, 'I have an altar with various figures of Buddhas. [...] In the morning I make little water offerings to the Buddha [...] I do that before I do my meditation. Then I do three **prostrations** and sit down and try to concentrate.'

The Buddha is not treated as a god, but is respected as a special teacher who laid out the way to Enlightenment. People make offerings as a way of thanking him for his guidance. At a shrine, offering bowls are provided so that they can give such things as water, flowers and light (in the form of candles)to the Buddha. Flowers remind Buddhists about anicca: nothing is permanent and even beautiful flowers fade and die. Lighted candles remind them of Enlightenment. Water symbolizes purity, clarity and calmness.

There is no standard architectural style for temples. Some temples in Britain are in disused churches. In the temple, monks often lead worship, chanting from scriptures or **mantras**, which are words to meditate on and focus the mind. The lay Buddhists take part by meditating and repeating the monks' chants.

b Flowers are often left outside Buddhist temples like these offerings in Bangkok, Thailand.

Activities

1. A group of British Buddhists want to promote awareness and understanding of what worship means to Buddhists. Produce a clear and interesting guide to Buddhist worship for people who want to know more.

2. 'Worship without God or gods is impossible.' Write a response to this statement, using what you know about Buddhist worship.

3. Listen to some Buddhist chanting and say how it makes you feel.

Where do Buddhist Beliefs Come From?

Objectives

- Identify the features of a product that fits in with the teachings of the Buddha
- Make clear reference to the Noble Eightfold Path and the Five Precepts
- Explain why Buddhists would approve of the product

Task

You have been approached by an ethical company that wants to make a product that will appeal to Buddhist purchasers.

a Decide on the product. It must do no harm to living things or the environment, in use or the way it's made, and must also take into account the Noble Eightfold Path and the Five Precepts. Be prepared to justify your choice with reference to Buddhist teachings.

b Design a marketing booklet that will accompany the product in which you explain clearly, using the Noble Eightfold Path and the Five Precepts, why it will appeal to Buddhists.

A bit of guidance...

Aim to show your understanding of Buddhist teaching as well as market the product. Ask yourself these questions: How important is it to live a life that causes no harm? How easy is it to live an ethical life? Note down your views so that you can share and discuss them.

Hints and tips

To help you tackle this task, you could:

- decide what type of product is to be marketed. Is it a food, toy, computer game, cosmetic? Or something else?
- think about how it is produced, how much is paid to the people who make it and how much it will be sold for.

? What does this symbol mean?

Guidance

What level are you aiming at? Have a look at the grid below to see what you need to do to achieve that level. What would you need to do to improve your work?

	I can...
Level 3	• give brief descriptions of the Noble Eightfold Path and Five Precepts using the correct religious vocabulary • begin to identify the impact of these teachings on people's lives • express my own views about the importance of ethical living.
Level 4	• show a clear understanding of the Noble Eightfold Path and Five Precepts, referring to religious sources • give examples of the correct way for Buddhists to behave • recognize and describe how Buddhists' beliefs affect their actions • express my opinion about the value and challenges of ethical living.
Level 5	• show clear understanding of the Noble Eightfold Path and Five Precepts using specific religious vocabulary • explain why these beliefs are important to those who follow them and give examples • present my work in a clear and relevant way • express and evaluate my own views about the challenges of ethical living.
Level 6	• describe and explain the Noble Eightfold Path and Five Precepts, referring to religious sources and using a wide range of religious vocabulary • show how these concepts are still relevant for Buddhists today • present my work in an interesting, structured and coherent way • critically evaluate my own responses to the challenges of ethical living.

Ready for more?

When you have completed this task, you can also work on your skills for Levels 6 and 7, and perhaps even higher. This is an extension task.

In this unit you have looked at many teachings that advise Buddhists on the right way to live their lives. Compare and contrast Buddhist teachings about how to live with teachings from another faith. Comment on the similarities and differences that you find, and discuss whether or not you agree with the teachings about how to live that are presented by these faiths. You could start by making a Venn diagram so that you can recognize similarities and differences more easily.

3.1 What does it Mean to Belong?

Learning Objectives

In this unit you will:

- define the importance of community to Buddhists
- explore the place of religious communities in society
- reflect on the different roles people play in a community.

Starter

- What do you understand by the word 'community'?
- What images come into your mind when you think of monks and nuns?

The Buddha realized the importance of good friends. When one of his followers said to him, 'This is half of the holy life – admirable friendship', the Buddha answered by saying that actually, admirable friendship is the whole of the holy life because when people have good friends, they are better equipped to pursue the Noble Eightfold Path. It is certainly true that good friends can help us through life and make it much more enjoyable.

The wider group of Buddhists, on a local and global scale, is called the Sangha. This word translates well into English as 'community'. Friendship and community are of great importance to Buddhists. They find safety and security in three things: the Buddha, the dhamma and the Sangha. These are often referred to as the **Three Refuges** or **Three Jewels**.

? What do you think the word 'refuge' means here?

? What kind of communities do you belong to?

For some Buddhists, the Sangha is the community of monks (**bhikkhus**) and nuns (**bhikkhunis**). These people dedicate their lives to Buddhism and feel that monastic life, without the distractions of living in the lay community, makes it easier to reach Enlightenment. They live very simply. They have no possessions and do not place much value in the things around them. They make and follow over 250 different vows, which make up a code of guidelines called the Vinaya pitaka.

d Buddhist boys receive food from upsakas.

Case Study

Mrs Harvey is a lay Buddhist. She visits the temple when she can, and is very much a part of the Buddhist community. She says, 'I enjoy coming [to the temple] because we all meet up with friends and enjoy the food, and I join my friends to pray to Buddha.'

Useful Words

Bikkhu Buddhist monk
Bikkhuni Buddhist nun
Ordained Those who in Buddhism, train to be and are made into monks and nuns
Three Refuges/Three Jewels The three most precious things in Buddhism: the Buddha, the dhamma, the Sangha
Upsaka A member of the lay Buddhist community

Not all Buddhists are **ordained** as monks and nuns. Many describe the Sangha as the whole community of Buddhists around the world. Lay Buddhists, those who are not monks or nuns, are called **upsakas**. They promise to keep to the Five Precepts and support the bhikkhus by providing them with clothing and food. In return, the bhikkhus provide teaching and guidance to the upsakas. This helps everyone, builds good kamma, and increases the sense of community within the Sangha.

Reflection

The poet John Donne wrote, 'No man is an island'. What does this quotation tell you about community?

Activities

1 a If you were to go and stay in a Buddhist monastery for a few days, which of the Five Precepts would you find most difficult to keep? Explain why. What do you think is the value of the Five Precepts?

b What might a Buddhist learn from spending some time living in a monastery? What might **you** learn from it?

2 The Buddha said that admirable friendship was the whole of the holy life. Write a story or create a cartoon that shows the importance of friendship to Buddhists and explores the idea of friends helping each other on the Noble Eightfold Path (see Unit 2.3).

3 Prepare questions ready to interview Mrs Harvey about the importance of her relationship with ordained Buddhists.

3.2 Same Faith, Different Ways

Learning Objectives

In this unit you will:

- identify examples of diversity in Buddhist belief and practice
- explain how Buddhists from different traditions aim for the same goal
- reflect on whether unity can be found despite differences in practice.

Starter

- List lots of different types of music. What do they have in common?

Buddhism is a faith with many traditions throughout the world. Buddhists practise their faith in different ways depending on which teachings they follow, where they live and who taught them. One type of Buddhism is not considered to be better than any other. They are just different ways of following the same path.

There are two main traditions of Buddhism. After the Buddha's death, his closest followers met to decide on the exact wording of his teachings. About a hundred years later there was another meeting, where people disagreed on how to interpret the Buddha's teachings. Those who accepted the original interpretation became known as the Elders. Gradually the Way of the Elders became the **Theravada** school of Buddhism. The **Mahayana** (Great Vehicle) school arose from those who disagreed with the Elders.

There are now almost 400 million Buddhists who live in many different countries. The majority live in Asia and the Far East. In the twentieth century, Buddhism spread to the Western world and the number of Buddhists in Europe and North America is increasing.

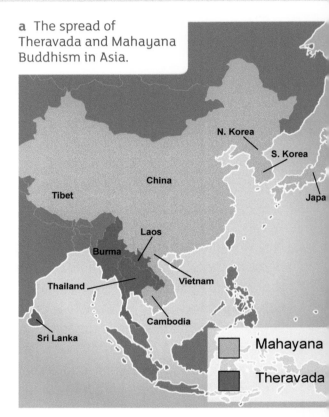

a The spread of Theravada and Mahayana Buddhism in Asia.

N. Korea
S. Korea
China
Japan
Tibet
Laos
Burma
Vietnam
Thailand
Cambodia
Sri Lanka

Mahayana
Theravada

Case Study

Mrs Aldam goes to the Jamyang Buddhist Centre in South London, where they follow the Mahayana tradition. There is a teacher from Tibet who teaches the people about the Buddha. But as Mrs Aldam says, they do 'all sorts of things – meditation classes, yoga classes – a lot of things besides [learning about] the straight teaching of the Buddha'.

Useful Words

Bodhisattva Wise Buddhists who keep coming back to the world after they die to help others
Mahayana The Great Vehicle; one of two main schools of Buddhism
Theravada The Way of the Elders; one of two main schools of Buddhism

The Mahayana tradition has spread more widely, making up the majority of the world's Buddhists. As it spread through different countries, it adapted to the local cultures. There are therefore various forms of Mahayana Buddhism, such as Zen, Pure Land, and Tibetan Buddhism (see Units 3.4, 3.5 and 4.2).

There is not as much emphasis on the monastic way of life for some Mahayana Buddhists. They follow the teachings of the sacred texts called the Pali Canon, but the Heart and Diamond Sutras are also very important. Mahayana Buddhists place great value in the **bodhisattva**, wise Buddhists who keep coming back to the world after they die to help others.

Theravada Buddhism seeks to follow the original teaching of the Buddha, the Pali Canon. A simple life of meditation is very important to Theravada Buddhists and many prefer the monastic life so they can follow the Buddha's teachings more closely. The monks and nuns wear saffron robes, probably because this yellow-orange dye was once the cheapest. The monks and nuns teach the lay people, who give them food in return.

c Young Theravada Buddhists set out to collect food in Burma.

b

? This picture shows a bodhisattva. Make a list of the qualities you think a bodhisattva should have. ⎓〰⎓

Reflection

Think back to your responses to the starter questions. Is variety in life a good thing? Think about times when it is and times when it could cause conflict.

Activities

1 From what you know about Buddhism, how can a Buddhist belief help people to be united?

2 'What unites us is greater than what divides us.' This quotation is attributed to John F. Kennedy. Do you think this could be true of Buddhism? Explain your thinking.

3 Mrs Aldam says that she benefits a lot from going to the Buddhist centre. Find out about the work of a Buddhist centre in your area and write a newspaper article about what they do.

Let's Meet a Monk

Learning Objectives

In this unit you will:

- identify why people become Buddhist monks and nuns
- explore and evaluate the life of a Theravada Buddhist monk
- reflect on the idea of committing your life to a community.

Starter

- What do you want to do with your life when you leave school? Why?

? Monk Boonyoung says, 'When I was younger, I wanted to be a racing driver.' What about you?

Case Study

Phra Aod Boonyoung has been a Theravada Buddhist monk for 16 years. He was given his Buddhist name by a senior monk when he was ordained. He lives at a Buddhist temple in Birmingham. He says, 'being a monk in Birmingham isn't difficult because it's such a multicultural city.'

How does being a monk affect your everyday life?

'Buddhist monks follow the Buddha's teachings (precepts). We have to be disciplined. Monks have 227 precepts. That is why we have to wear a robe and shave our heads. We teach people about Buddhism, but we can only reach the goal of Enlightenment on our own. It's not like other religions, where you are with other people who worship and share with each other. One has to practise by themselves to reach their goal, to walk along the path that is the Buddha's teaching.'

Wat Santiwongsaram Temple, Birmingham

b There are over 500 Buddhist groups and centres in Britain. Boonyoung belongs to the Wat Santiwongsaram Temple in Birmingham.

What is your routine?

'My routine is to wake up at half past five in the morning and sit in meditations for one hour. After that we help out around the monastery. If we have free time, then we practise meditation and observe our minds. At midday, we eat and then go to teach people to meditate. In the evenings, we chant again and do meditations for one hour, and chanting for half an hour.'

How do you spend your time?

'We pay respect to the Buddha, the founder of the dhamma. Dhamma are the rules that guide us to walk along the path.' The monks also travel around the country to share the teachings of the Buddha with other people. Sometimes, they are so much in demand that they only get to spend about one month a year in the temple!

How do people become monks?

'To become a monk, you have to start by following precepts. You also need to practise meditations. People who are interested in becoming monks come to the temple and read the scriptures, so that they can be introduced to Buddhism and how to become a Buddhist monk. If people want to become a Buddhist monk, then the Sangha (Buddhist community) will decide if that person can become a Buddhist monk. They cannot be ordained until they can practise and be accepted. Some people can stay for ten years and still not become a Buddhist monk!'

Reflection

What do you think you will be doing in 5, 10 and 15 years' time? Do you think you will be doing what you wanted to do with your life?

Activities

1. Using what you have discovered about Boonyoung and from your own research, make a poster that explains the life, duties and experiences of a Buddhist monk or nun in Britain.

2. If you could ask Boonyoung any questions, what would they be? Write a questionnaire to find out more about what it is like to be a monk.

3. Drawing on Boonyoung's experiences, write at least one diary entry from a Buddhist monk's perspective, explaining and exploring what monastic life is like.

3.4 Uncluttering Your Mind

Learning Objectives

In this unit you will:

- explore the importance of meditation to Buddhists
- analyse different meditation styles
- reflect on the experience of meditation.

Starter

- What is the person in the picture below doing?

- Is the idea of 'rising above' the world and its problems attractive to you?

Meditation often comes to mind when people think about Buddhism. It is a very important part of the faith. It has been said that imagining Buddhism without meditation is like imagining Christianity without God.

When Buddhists meditate, they are trying to get away from the busyness of life. They are not trying to reach a supernatural or mystical state. They are separating themselves from all the distractions around them, which might be specific things or their own thoughts. They are attempting simply to be fully focused and aware. In that way they hope to find calm, joy and clarity of thought.

This type of controlled concentration for significant lengths of time is difficult to achieve. It takes lots of practice to find the Right Mindfulness. The effect is very powerful. A focused mind can be thought of as like the light from a laser beam. When the light is spread over a large area, it is quite dim. But when it is focused, it is so strong it can cut through steel.

Focussing the mind can take many forms. Some Buddhists spend many days constructing sand **mandalas**, which requires intense concentration. Others, such as **Pure Land** Buddhists, chant and repeat certain words or phrases to focus the mind.

? What is this person doing?

b Sand mandalas can take huge amounts of time to make and are easily destroyed.

Useful Words

Mandala A sacred design within a circle
Pure Land A school of Buddhism that believes in reaching Enlightenment through meditation on Amida Buddha
Stupa A conical object that represents the Buddha's holy mind

In Pure Land Buddhism, a prominent school of Buddhism in Japan and China, meditation focuses on Amida Buddha, a different Buddha from Siddattha (see Unit 1.1). Pure Land Buddhists believe that Amida Buddha has an eternal realm, a 'pure land', where anyone who calls on his name in sincere faith can be reborn and work towards Enlightenment. And so, when these Buddhists meditate, they say the name of this Buddha repeatedly to seek rebirth in the pure land.

Reflection

How important are our thoughts?

Case Study

Mrs Aldam has a small room at home where she meditates. In it, she has some objects to help her focus. There is a Buddharupa, which represents the Buddha's holy body, and a **stupa**, which represents the Buddha's holy mind. She sometimes listens to a CD of the Buddha's teachings, which also helps her focus.

Molly says that meditation focuses her mind in her day-to-day life. She tries to meditate before school, so that she can go through the day feeling positive and with a clear mind. This helps her to be as kind as possible to other people. If Molly didn't meditate before school, then she feels that her brain would feel a bit cluttered.

'Life is available only in the present moment.'
Thich Nhat Hanh, *Taming the Tiger Within*

Activities

1. How can actions like the making of mandalas be a form of meditation? Which activities would help you focus your mind? When do you feel most focused?

2. In small groups, sit in a circle and spend five minutes in complete silence. Then, still in silence, write about the thoughts that were going through your mind, the things you heard and the way you felt. Share these with your group.

3. Molly says that meditation helps to unclutter her mind. In your own words, and using examples from this unit, explain how Buddhists use meditation.

Learning Objectives

In this unit you will:

- identify some of the beliefs and practices of Zen Buddhists
- analyse how Zen practices differ from other types of Buddhism
- reflect on what it means to 'live in the moment'.

Starter

- What is the sound of one hand clapping?

Zen Buddhism began in China and spread first to Korea, and then to Japan. It is also very popular in the West today.

'Zen' comes from a Sanskrit word meaning 'meditation' or 'concentration'. This shows that meditation is a very important part of Zen Buddhist practice, which comes from the belief that Enlightenment must come from within. It cannot just be learned from the scriptures or from taking part in worship. Instead, Zen Buddhists believe that Enlightenment is within everyone and all people have to do is realize that. They believe that if the mind is calm and relaxed, Enlightenment can be attained in a flash of insight without warning while a person is doing something very ordinary.

Zen Buddhism teaches that people should concentrate fully on every action they do. The action can be anything – mowing the lawn, brushing your teeth, tidying your room. It does not have to seem like a spiritual act, but it does need full commitment and thought. It is a form of meditation and you have to train your mind not to wander.

> *'All beings by nature are Buddhas as ice by nature is water. Apart from water there is no ice; apart from beings no Buddhas.'*
> Hakuin Ekaku, influential Zen teacher (1686–1768)

? Have you ever learned a skill that requires self-discipline? How difficult was it for you?

? Why do you think archery is used by Zen Buddhists as a form of meditation?

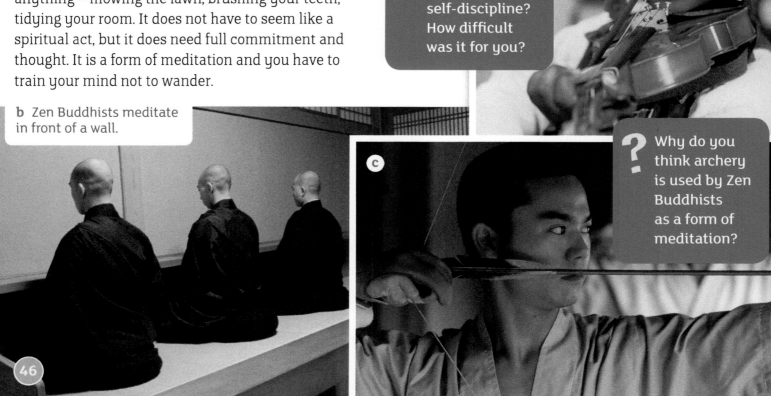

b Zen Buddhists meditate in front of a wall.

Zen Buddhists often focus their minds on one specific activity, such as tea-making or archery. Living in the moment and experiencing life in this focused way is essential to Zen Buddhism and brings overall calm. All Zen Buddhists practise **zazen**, which means 'seated meditation'. It is about opening the mind.

📄 *Reflection*

'Living in the moment is an easy thing to do.' Do you agree? Why?

d A Zen garden does not have flowers or leaves that change; the only change comes from how a person looks at the garden.

Some Zen Buddhists believe that meditation to calm the mind is enough, and face away from each other towards the wall to meditate. Others face one another to meditate, often on a **koan**, which is a question asked by a Zen master to a novice or trainee.

Koans are like riddles and often do not seem to make sense or have one clear, logical answer. But the aim is not to answer the koan. It is the meditative practice that someone goes through to reach a solution that is important.

One of the most famous koans was a Zen teacher asking his disciple to describe the sound of one hand clapping...

> 'Drink your tea slowly and reverently, as if it is the axis on which the world earth revolves – slowly, evenly, without rushing toward the future.'
> Thich Nhat Hanh, prominent Zen Buddhist

Useful Words

Zen Buddhism A school of Mahayana Buddhism

Activities

1. How might a Zen garden help a Buddhist to become calm and meditate?

2. How is Zen Buddhism different from the other forms of Buddhism you know about? Make a table to show the similarities and differences.

3. Do you agree that most people are used to clear and logical answers to questions? Research some koans and think about how to answer them.

Learning Objectives

In this unit you will:

- explore the link between meditation and happiness
- investigate the life of Matthieu Ricard
- reflect on the nature of happiness.

Starter

- What makes you happy?
- Do you think that happiness is a skill that can be learned?

Different things make people happy. While one person might find pure happiness in baking a cake, another person might find this dull or stressful.

Although happiness is relative, it can be scientifically measured. This involves using an MRI scanner to monitor brain activity. When there is a lot of activity in the left prefrontal cortex of the brain, the person is happy. In the happiest people, the right prefrontal cortex, which deals with negative feelings, is less active.

Apparently, Matthieu Ricard is the happiest person in the world. During tests on his brain, his positive emotions were much stronger than anybody else's ever tested.

Ricard was born in Paris. He excelled at school and then gained a **PhD** in molecular genetics. At the age of 30 he decided to dedicate his life to becoming a Tibetan Buddhist monk. He has written many books and conducted many scientific studies into happiness, but instead of becoming wealthy, he gives all the money he receives to charity. He supports 110 humanitarian projects, including hospitals, schools and care for the elderly. He has also been invited to speak at many international conferences and is often at United Nations meetings to promote happiness.

He lives at the Shechen Tennyi Dargyeling Monastery in Nepal and is the French translator for the Dalai Lama (see Unit 4.3).

'Our life can be greatly transformed by even a minimal change in how we manage our thoughts and perceive and interpret the world. Happiness is a skill. It requires effort and time.'
Matthieu Ricard

? Do you think this is the happiest man in the world? Why?

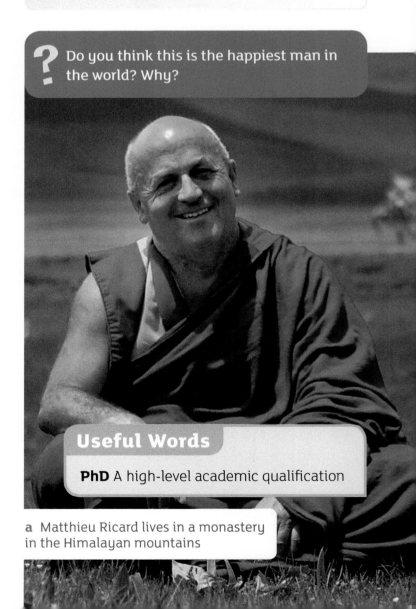

Useful Words

PhD A high-level academic qualification

a Matthieu Ricard lives in a monastery in the Himalayan mountains

'The route to happiness in many ways is contentment: not regretting what happened yesterday or hoping that something good will happen tomorrow, but living in the moment.'
Matthieu Ricard

c

b Ricard is a translator for the Dalai Lama at public events, such as this press conference in Paris in 2008.

Some people believe that Ricard is so happy because of the amount of time he spends meditating. Many scientific studies find clear links between meditation and improvements in health and happiness. Matthieu Ricard could be clear evidence for this as he has spent over 10,000 hours in meditation. He believes that, with training, happiness can be taught and learned.

Ricard has a website and a blog where he keeps people informed about what he is doing. He clearly thinks that a Buddhist way of life increases happiness. One blog entry is titled, 'The ten things we think will make us happier, but don't'. Then he lists things such as wanting to be rich and famous. Instead he proposes a Buddhist Middle Way that gets away from statements such as 'I want' and 'I need'.

? How do you think you might train yourself to be happier?

Reflection
Do you think happiness comes from inside or outside? Think about the things that make you happy.

Activities

1 Using the information here and from his website, create a biography entry for Ricard. Make sure that you include some of his quotations and make clear links to his Buddhist practice. You could also include some of his photographs.

2 Ricard would certainly agree that 'money does not buy happiness', but his work has made a

lot of money that he gives to good causes. In groups, plan a play to show how money can make people more and less happy. Be ready to perform your play if asked.

3 Write a letter from a Buddhist to a non-Buddhist friend to explain how following the Middle Way (Unit 2.3) can bring happiness.

Belonging to the Buddhist Faith

Objectives

- Explain the commitments and lifestyle of Buddhist monks and nuns
- Reflect on and evaluate your own character and ideas about life
- Compare your views with the Buddhist lifestyles you have studied.

Task

Draw on your learning about the commitments and lifestyle of Buddhist monks and nuns to answer these questions.

1 What is life like for a Buddhist monk or nun? Describe and explain the commitments made by bhikkhus. You can explore this within any strand of Buddhism.

2 Could you imagine ever being a Buddhist monk or nun? Reflect on your own character and beliefs to answer the question carefully.

You can choose how to present your responses. For example, you could write an essay, a letter to a friend, a series of diary entries or make a presentation.

? Becoming or monk or nun involves following many rules. Do you think that you could do that?

A bit of guidance...

Aim to show your understanding of the commitment and lifestyle in ordained Buddhist communities, as well as giving your own views.

Hints and tips

To help you tackle this task, you could:

- make a table to show clearly what monks and nuns do with their time, and provide a useful basis for your work

- do some research on individual monks and nuns to understand their personal experience of monastic life better

- ask your friends or family what you are like to live with!

Guidance

What level are you aiming at? Have a look at the grid below to see what you need to do to achieve that level. What would you need to do to improve your work?

	I can...
Level 3	• use religious vocabulary to describe some of the commitments and lifestyles of Buddhist monks and nuns • explore and explain my own views.
Level 4	• use a range of religious vocabulary to describe and explain some of the commitments and lifestyles of Buddhist monks and nuns • reflect on this way of life and explore and explain my own views and reasons in some detail.
Level 5	• use a wide range of religious vocabulary to describe and evaluate the commitments and lifestyles of Buddhist monks and nuns • give reasons as to why this way of life is important to ordained Buddhist communities • justify and evaluate my own views and reasons in some detail.
Level 6	• use a wide range of religious vocabulary accurately and with confidence to explore and evaluate the commitments and lifestyles of Buddhist monks and nuns • give reasons and examples of why this way of life is important to ordained Buddhist communities • justify and critically evaluate my own views and responses to the lifestyles of Buddhist monks and nuns in some detail • compare and contrast my own views with Buddhist opinions.

Ready for more?

When you have completed this task, you can also work on your skills for Levels 6 and 7, and perhaps even higher. This is an extension task.

In addition to Buddhist ways of life and your own reflections, you could go on to research, explain and evaluate the commitments and lifestyles of religious communities of at least one (ideally two) other faiths such as Christianity and Hinduism. You could also question your friends, families and teachers about their views on community living. Finally, compare and contrast your findings with some of the Buddhist ways of life you have studied.

Learning Objectives

In this unit you will:

- identify why the King of Bhutan took his people's happiness so seriously
- identify what features determine Gross National Happiness
- reflect on what Gross National Happiness might mean in Britain today.

Starter

Is the happiness of a nation as important as the happiness of an individual?

In 1972, in the Buddhist kingdom of Bhutan, King Jigme Singye Wangchuck introduced the concept of Gross National Happiness (**GNH**). The king had introduced a process of modernization and, as a Buddhist, he knew that happiness could not be measured purely by how much money Bhutan had.

The idea for the term 'Gross National Happiness' came from the similarly named 'Gross Domestic Product' (**GDP**). Many countries are measured by their GDP, which is the total value of all goods and services produced in an economy. The GDP of a country is often linked to its standard of living. In theory, the higher the GDP, the higher the standard of living.

'Gross national happiness is more impovrtant than gross national product.'
King Jigme Singye Wangchuck

? What do you think the king meant by this?

a King Jigme Singye Wangchuck of Bhutan believed Buddhist priciples made for a happier kingdom.

b This map shows Bhutan and the surrounding countries.

Bhutan is a Buddhist kingdom, governed by spiritual values, and the king wanted it to keep its unique character. For this reason, GNH rests on four principles:

- promotion of sustainable development
- preservation and promotion of cultural values
- conservation of the natural environment
- establishment of good governance.

The idea was that this would encourage spiritual and material development in Bhutan to happen at the same time. Any laws passed in Bhutan have to take GNH into account.

China

Tibet

Nepal

Bhutan

India

Bangladesh

Burma

c This photograph of a group of young boys at play shows why GNH is important in Bhutan.

d The introduction of television brought many new and foreign concepts to the attention of the people of Bhutan.

Interestingly, social problems began to occur in Bhutan after 1999. The king lifted a ban on television and suddenly the people were exposed to things that they had never seen before. They were offered many channels, including American shows that featured violence and crime. Television became incredibly popular, but the change in attitudes and behaviour was overwhelming. The sudden rise in crime was blamed on the introduction of television and values that did not fit in with the Buddhist principles of this peaceful kingdom. Even so, Bhutan's emphasis on GNH still attracts the interest and admiration of many countries worldwide.

Reflection

Do you agree that GNH is more important than GDP? Does having more money or things always lead to greater happiness? Why or why not?

Activities

1 The king said that the purpose of GNH was to achieve a balance between the spiritual and the material. Why would he, as a Buddhist, think that was important?

2 **a** What would make Britain a happier place right now? With a partner, make a list and explain each point.

b Imagine that you are the prime minister of Great Britain. Prepare a speech to deliver to your class, explaining how you plan to raise our GNH as a nation.

3 Some people think the introduction of television into Bhutan had a negative effect on people's behaviour. Do you think that there is any link between what shows we watch and what we do?

4.2 Faith Under Pressure

Learning Objectives

In this unit you will:

- explain why some Buddhists get involved in political conflicts
- examine whether political activity is in line with Buddhist teaching
- reflect on your own attitudes to challenging injustice.

Starter

- What things in life do you think are worth defending?
- Have you ever stood up to a bully? What happened?

Buddhists generally lead peaceful lives, but sometimes, like the Tibetan and Burmese Buddhists, they encounter conflicts with others.

Tibet has been a Buddhist country since the seventh century (when the religion was introduced by Buddhists from India). Tibetan Buddhists value the relationship between teacher (or **lama**) and students greatly, so much so that the person who leads the country spiritually and politically is called the Dalai Lama. This teacher-student relationship is so important that they added a fourth Refuge or Jewel to the traditional three (see Unit 3.1): 'I go to the lama for refuge.'

The current Dalai Lama, Tenzin Gyatso, is Tibetan but doesn't live in Tibet because in 1950, the Chinese invaded. Tibetans felt increasingly threatened, and so, 300, 000 Tibetans surrounded the palace in 1959 to protect the Dalai Lama. However, this peaceful uprising couldn't last against armed forces, and so the Dalai Lama left Tibet. Even though Gyatso still lives in exile in India, he continues to stand up for the need for peaceful solutions to violent situations, and wants Tibet to become a 'zone of peace'.

> **?** What aspects of Buddhist teachings and beliefs might make it hard for a Buddhist to decide to take part in political protests?

> '*Hatred will not cease by hatred, but by love alone.*'
> Tenzin Gyatso, the Dalai Lama

a This photograph was taken in front of the United Nations Headquarters, New York, in 1959. The men are trying to gain support for Tibet.

> '*I will not harm living things.*'
> First Precept

FREE AMERICA HELP KEEP TIBET FREE

PROTECT THE DALAI LAMA FROM RED

1776 DECLARATION of INDEPENDENCE of U.S.A., 1959 of TIBET

b The current Dalai Lama promotes a peaceful approach to resolving conflict.

In Burma, the majority of the population follows Theravada Buddhism. There have been a number of occasions when the people of Burma have felt that they had to protest against injustice in their society. For example, in 1988 thousands of people, including students and many monks were killed, arrested, and tortured for protesting against the military government.

More recently, the famous Buddhist politician and peace campaigner, Aung San Suu Kyi, leader of the National League for Democracy, led her party to a landslide victory in the 1990 Burmese elections. The military regime ignored the election result and Aung San Suu Kyi was arrested. She spent 14 years in detention, mostly under house arrest. During this time, she left her house to pray with Buddhist monks who had gathered outside her gate. She asked people around the world: 'Please use your liberty to promote ours.' Suu Kyi was released in 2010 and is still the leader of her political party.

c

Useful Words

Lama A spiritual leader in Tibetan Buddhism

d Aung San Suu Kyi won the Nobel Peace Prize in 2007.

> Non-violence means positive action. You have to work for whatever you want. [...] It just means that the methods you use are not violent ones. Some people think that non-violence is passiveness. It's not so.

Reflection

How would you feel if you had to live in exile from your own country? What would you miss about your life at home?

Activities

1. Write a letter from a Buddhist in the UK to Aung San Suu Kyi when she was under house arrest, giving her support and encouragement.

2. 📄 Write an article for a British newspaper about Suu Kyi leaving her house to pray with the monks. Think about who to interview, how to write the story and which facts and details to include. Include your own opinion.

3. Imagine you are the Dalai Lama and have just fled Tibet for exile in India. Prepare a speech to the Tibetan people to explain why you left, how you reached India and what you intend to do now. Make sure you include Buddhist teachings about non-violence in your speech.

Learning Objectives

In this unit you will:

- explore the life and philosophy of Tenzin Gyatso
- examine the impact of his teachings on people's lives
- reflect on and evaluate his wisdom.

Starter

- Who is the wisest person you know?
- What makes them so wise?

Tenzin Gyatso, the 14th Dalai Lama, is known around the world for his wisdom, which often challenges the way people live. In 1989, he won the Nobel Peace Prize for his work on promoting peace, and has won numerous other awards over his lifetime.

The Dalai Lama is also known for his contagious humour and good nature even though he has had to endure great hardships in life. His outlook on life is the result of personal experience.

The Dalai Lama's current home is at a monastery in Dharamsala, in northern India. He always dresses simply in his robes, but he travels the world to give talks and share his wisdom with others, and has met many world leaders and celebrities. Because Buddhism is not a faith with lots of rules and regulations, the Dalai Lama and his teachings appeal to a broad range of people.

> 'My religion is very simple. My religion is kindness.'
>
> 'This is my simple religion. There is no need for temples; no need for complicated philosophy. Our own brain, our own heart is our temple; the philosophy is kindness.'
>
> 'All major religious traditions carry basically the same message, that is love, compassion and forgiveness. The important thing is they should be part of our daily lives.'
>
> Tenzin Gyatso, the Dalai Lama

a At the main Tibetan monastery in India, teachings are often given in several languages.

b The Dalai Lama met Prince Charles on a visit to London.

Dalai Lama on how to live

'Happiness is not something ready made. It comes from your own actions.'

'Every day, think as you wake up, today I am fortunate to be alive, I have a precious human life, I am not going to waste it. I am going to use all my energies to develop myself, to expand my heart out to others; to achieve Enlightenment for the benefit of all beings. I am going to have kind thoughts towards others, I am not going to get angry or think badly about others. I am going to benefit others as much as I can.'

'Remember that, sometimes, not getting what you want is a wonderful stroke of luck.'

'Take into account that great love and great achievements involve great risk.'

Tenzin Gyatso, the Dalai Lama

c Tenzin Gyatso has been Dalai Lama for over 60 years.

Case Study

When Molly went to see the Dalai Lama teach in Manchester, she was given blessing strings. Buddhists sometimes wear them around their necks or wrists. Molly says, 'It has been blessed by the Dalai Lama and there is a knot in the string that is part of the blessing.' Her grandmother adds, 'We are supposed to keep them on until they fall off.' Many Buddhists think that the significance of the teaching will stay with the person who wears the string.

Reflection

Molly has her blessing strings. Do you have anything that you wear or keep with you to remind you of something or someone that's important to you?

Activities

1 Choose one of the quotations from the Dalai Lama. Design a motivational poster for your school based on the quotation.

2 'Take into account that great love and great achievements involve great risk.' Do you agree? Think about specific people who have risked a lot to achieve a lot. Present a case study of one of these people, explaining how they have lived up to this quotation.

3 Prepare a speech welcoming the Dalai Lama to your school and introducing him. Explain who he is, what he believes in and what he has done.

Learning Objectives

In this unit you will:

- explain Buddhist teaching on craving
- explore if it is possible for the modern world to learn from those teachings
- reflect on your own attitude to wanting and having things.

Starter

- 'I shop, therefore I am.' What do you think this means?
- Does what you buy, eat and wear affect who you are?

Consumerism is society's preoccupation with buying goods and services. Many countries around the world, especially in the West, are often thought of as being driven by consumerism. For example, the British fashion industry is worth £32 billion a year. People love buying things, and the Internet has made buying even quicker and easier. In some ways that is good, but people are often spending money they don't have on things they don't need!

The desire to have things, often instantly, has led to a global debt disaster in recent years. For example, personal debt in England now amounts to about a trillion pounds. Can an ancient faith like Buddhism have anything to say about such a modern challenge?

a Can you remember being desperate to buy something?

'The impulse "I want!" and the impulse "I'll have" – lose them! That is where most people get stuck; without those, you can use your eyes to guide you through this suffering state.'
The Buddha, *Suttanipāta 706*

? Do you ever have these impulses? What encourages people to think like this?

The Second Noble Truth of Buddhism is that dukkha (see Unit 1.3) is caused by cravings and desires. The more people have, the more they want – a circle of desiring and craving. As a result, they become trapped because they are never satisfied. The Buddha taught the Middle Way – a life between the extremes of self-indulgence and self-denial.

Case Study

Molly thinks that living in a consumer society is unsustainable. She says, 'it uses up resources and relies on exploitation of workers overseas. [...] To be overwhelmed by lots of different things we could have makes us quite dissatisfied and agitated. [...] Being a Buddhist means I am not so influenced by others who want certain products and fashions. [...] If I get something that I really desire, eventually the pleasure will fade and it will be boring and I will start to want something else.'

Tom says, 'the teachings of the Buddha do help me to care less about belongings'. He says that even if you have paid lots of money for something, it is still just an impermanent item and if it gets broken, it can be replaced.

Activities

1. Write an article for a fashion magazine about consumerism seen from a Buddhist point of view.

2. Molly says, 'If I get something I want, it won't actually give me the satisfaction I think it will.' Has this happened to you? Write a story about something that you really wanted but that you were disappointed with when you got it.

3. Prepare your arguments either for or against the statement, 'Consumerism is bad.' To help you start thinking about the issues, look at the labels in some of your clothes and see where they were made.

Reflection

'All I want, I'll have.' How influenced are you by this impulse?

4.5 Is Buddhism Compatible with Science?

Learning Objectives

In this unit you will:

- examine Buddhist responses to the scientific view of the world
- ask questions about the relationship between science and faith
- reflect on your own views about faith and science.

Starter

- Do you think there can ever be a positive relationship between science and faith?
- What can the two learn from each other?

Although faith and science do have things in common, it has become increasingly popular to suggest that they are opposites that don't go well together. Some people say that they cannot believe in religion because they believe in science. For example, the popular scientist Richard Dawkins has written a book called *The God Delusion*, which argues that a supernatural 'creator' cannot exist. He also presented television shows based on the lack of scientific evidence for God.

Buddhism seems to have responded positively to the advances in technology and modern scientific discoveries. In 2012, the current Dalai Lama was awarded the prestigious Templeton Prize, primarily for his work on the relationship between science and faith.

One of the main areas that the Dalai Lama has been involved in is **neuroscience**, and Buddhism has played a part in developing a clearer understanding in this area. One neuroscientist from the University of Madison was so inspired by the Dalai Lama that he opened a centre within the university for investigating healthy minds. The centre employs scientists to discover more about the mind and how we can be healthier and happier.

'For decades, Tenzin Gyatso, the 14th Dalai Lama, has vigorously focused on the connections between the investigative traditions of science and Buddhism as a way to better understand and advance what both disciplines might offer the world.'
Templeton Foundation

'I am studying modern science because I believe it can help me understand my Buddhism better.'
Unknown Tibetan Buddhist Monk, from research by Professor Arri Eisen, Emory University

? Can you think of other ways faith could help us understand science, or vice versa?

Useful Words

Neuroscience Studies that focus on the structure and function of the brain and nervous system

a Richard Dawkins' books seem to suggest that faith and science are not compatible.

Buddhism does not take its beliefs primarily from scripture. Buddhists think that experience and reason are just as important, if not more so. Therefore, if science proves that something is true, such as the fact that the Earth moves around the Sun (which is not what some early traditional Buddhist scriptures say), then a Buddhist should accept the scientific perspective. It is this kind of attitude that has made many people think that Buddhism and science can be compatible.

In Buddhism, what exists is defined as what can be known. This fits very well with modern physics. But although Buddhism and modern science can work together, Buddhism is much more than a faith that is compatible with science. The Buddha taught that it is important to 'see' or realize things in the right way and this self-understanding goes much further than modern science can.

c This computer model shows how human nerve cells behave.

? Does knowing more about science take away the mystery and wonder of the world, or add to it?

b

Activities

1. Write a short paragraph in your own words, summarizing the relationship between science and Buddhism.

2. The Dalai Lama said that if something is supported by reason then we must accept it, but if something is unreasonable, we do not have to accept it. Is this a good view? Discuss this in pairs and make bullet points.

3. Do you think modern Britain is more of a scientific society or more of a religious society? Why?

Reflection

It is frequently said that religion is the enemy of science. Do you think that the two can ever really work together effectively?

4. Write a letter to Richard Dawkins from a Buddhist perspective explaining why you think that science and religion are more compatible than some people think. You could also mention views from other faiths you have studied.

Raising Questions, Exploring Answers

Objectives

- Evaluate and explain the place of Buddhism in the modern world
- Reflect on the history and heritage of Buddhism
- Develop interesting ways of presenting your learning about Buddhism

Task

Prepare a presentation for an assembly on the theme 'Buddhism: religion of the future'. Use what you have learned about the development of Buddhism and how it is practised in the modern world. Explain what it can teach the modern world about the way we live now and how we might live in the future. Create some interesting visual resources to make your presentation more engaging.

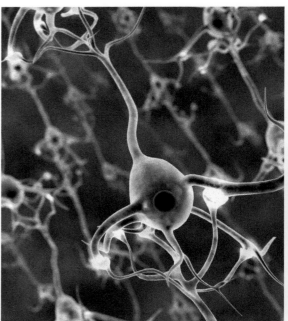

A bit of guidance...

The great scientist Albert Einstein (1879–1955) thought that Buddhism had the potential to be 'a religion of the future'. He explained that it would appeal to people because:

- it went beyond a belief in a personal God
- it didn't make complex and sweeping claims about its beliefs
- it focused on the natural and spiritual aspects of life
- it emphasized that the natural and spiritual world are at one.

You are going to show how Buddhism has adapted to the modern world and how it is a relevant faith for today.

Hints and tips

To help you tackle this task, you could:

- give specific examples of how Buddhism has engaged with modern issues
- research famous Buddhists and collect quotations from them about how their faith impacts their lives
- prepare some film clips to show how Buddhism can have positive effects on modern life.

Guidance

What level are you aiming at? Have a look at the grid below to see what you need to do to achieve that level. What would you need to do to improve your work?

	I can...
Level 3	• identify some important Buddhist beliefs • use religious vocabulary to describe how these beliefs relate to the modern world • respond thoughtfully to my learning to create an interesting presentation.
Level 4	• use a range of religious vocabulary to describe and explain some Buddhist beliefs • make links showing how these beliefs are relevant in the modern world • reflect on these beliefs and show how they could be applied to specific situations.
Level 5	• use a wide range of religious vocabulary and a variety of religious sources to describe and evaluate some Buddhist beliefs • make clear links between ancient beliefs and their relevance in the modern world • show understanding of more than one point of view • reflect on and evaluate the place of Buddhism in the world today.
Level 6	• use a wide range of religious vocabulary and sources accurately and with confidence to explore and evaluate Buddhist beliefs • explain clearly how the underlying principles behind these beliefs are relevant in the modern world • critically evaluate and explain how Buddhism is an evolving faith.

Ready for more?

When you have completed this task, you can also work on your skills for Levels 6 and 7, and perhaps even higher. This is an extension task.

Have other faiths adapted as well to the modern world as Buddhism? Find out about at least one other faith, and the contributions that it has made to the modern world. Produce a leaflet that shows comparisons between modern-day Buddhism and one or more other faiths.

Learning Objectives

In this unit you will:

- examine the growth of Buddhism in Britain
- evaluate the place of Buddhism in modern Britain
- reflect on Britain as a **multifaith** society.

Starter

- Are you someone who likes to fit in or stand out from the crowd?
- What might be the positive and negative aspects of being a Buddhist in Britain today?

To some extent, the country people live in shapes the way they behave. For instance, they have to follow the laws of that country and often keep its customs and traditions without even thinking about it. However, most people in Britain feel able to follow the religion of their choice or not have a religion at all.

Britain is now a **multicultural**, multifaith society. In the 2011 Census, 12% fewer people in England and Wales said they were Christians than in the 2001 Census. In contrast, the number of people who said they were Buddhist, Hindu, Jewish, Muslim or Sikh rose. In 2011 there were around 248,000 Buddhists, 72% more than in 2001.

Buddhism was introduced to Britain in the late nineteenth century and the Buddhist Society of Great Britain and Ireland was formed in 1924. There was another rise in popularity in the late twentieth century, when there was an increased interest in spirituality. In addition, more travel and communication between Asia and the UK meant that Buddhist teachings could spread to more places, more quickly.

'The problems we face today, violent conflicts, destruction of nature, poverty, hunger and so on are human-created problems which can be resolved through human effort, understanding and the development of brotherhood and sisterhood. We need to cultivate a universal response for one another and the planet we share.'

The Dalai Lama on the importance of interfaith dialogue

a The Dalai Lama believes strongly in the value of interfaith activity throughout the world.

Many people were attracted to Buddhism because it offered an alternative to other religions and traditions that they considered to be out of touch with modern life. Buddhism is sometimes described as a way of life, and many people choose to follow it without necessarily calling themselves religious.

To be a British Buddhist today does not require you to attend a place of worship, but lots of Buddhists do choose to attend a temple or community centre so that they can meet with other Buddhists for encouragement and learn more about their faith. **Retreats** are also popular. There are a number of monasteries around Britain that host organized retreats to help people develop a clearer understanding of Buddhism in a way that is relevant to life in modern Britain.

Case Study

Tom says 'where I live [in north Wales] there isn't a vast Buddhist community so not many people quite understand it. I've never been challenged on it but it's always been poked fun at, in a comical way.'

b Monks and lay people come together to worship and participate in Buddhist ceremonies at a temple in London.

Useful Words

Multicultural A society that contains several different cultural groups

Multifaith Something that involves a variety of faiths

Retreat A withdrawal from everyday life for a period of quiet thoughtfulness, usually in a monastery

Activities

① What aspects of Buddhism do you think might appeal to people in Britain and why?

② Find out about One World Week. In a group, plan events and activities to celebrate it at your school. If you could invite any Buddhist you like – living or dead – to be one of the main speakers, who would you choose and why?

Reflection

Do you agree with the Dalai Lama that if religious leaders would unite and talk to each other, the world's problems could be solved? How could this happen? What might help or hinder such unity?

Learning Objectives

In this unit you will:

- identify how Buddhists approach important stages in life
- analyse what it means to grow up as a Buddhist
- reflect on the importance of equality.

Starter

- Do you feel that everybody in your school is equal?
- How do you mark special occasions in your life?

Buddhists do not generally have big ceremonies to celebrate a child's birth, but in some Buddhist countries, such as Tibet, parents take their children to a monastery and ask their lama, or teacher, to choose a name that has a special meaning. Parents can also take their children to the local monastery to receive teaching from the monks and nuns.

In Theravada Buddhism, a boy might spend a while living in the monastery as a monk. He will have his head shaved and live like all the other monks. Some boys decide that they want to be ordained. For others, it reminds them that they are members of the Sangha whether ordained or not.

Although some Buddhists think it is easier to follow the Buddhist path as a single person, many others get married. There are no specifically Buddhist ceremonies for marriage. Buddhists usually follow the laws and customs of the country they live in.

a Young Buddhist boys often spend some time living and being taught in a monastery.

Married couples and families are welcome to visit the temple. Some might even stay in retreat in a monastery for a short time. In many Buddhist marriages, the man and the woman have equal responsibility for bringing up the children according to the Buddha's teachings. In a Buddhist family, relationships are guided by the Middle Way and the Five Precepts (see Unit 2.4) and should therefore be based on love and compassion.

Equality is an important concept in Buddhism. The Buddha's first followers included women as well as men. That was unusual, because in Indian society at that time, a woman's role was to be a wife and a mother, and to run the household. But Buddhist women, as well as men, can usually be ordained. Only cultural reasons, rather than the Buddha's teachings, would make that impossible. The Buddha taught that Enlightenment was available to everyone, male or female.

b Buddhist temples are often open to anyone who wants to include Buddhist principles in their lives and relationships.

c Women, such as these Burmese nuns, have the same opportunity to be ordained in Buddhism as men.

Reflection

'What people are on the inside is much more important than how they look on the outside.' Do you agree?

Activities

1 Why do you think that Buddhists don't usually have specific ceremonies to mark important stages in life?

2 Do you think that equality is important? Where around you can you see inequality? Find out what the other people in your class think and, in small groups, write a play script based around inequality. One of your characters must be a Buddhist.

3 Use your knowledge of the Middle Way and the Five Precepts to write a short guide to relationships in a Buddhist family.

5.3 How Much is Enough?

Learning Objectives

In this unit you will:

- explain what Buddhism teaches about wealth and poverty
- analyse some of the Buddha's teachings about money
- reflect on what it means to be rich or poor.

Starter

- Draw a quick sketch of a rich person. What shows that they are rich?
- How much is enough?

'How much is enough?' is a difficult question to answer. The average income for a family with two working parents in Britain is £40,000. To some people, that sounds like a lot of money. For others, it is not enough. What does Buddhism have to say about money and how we use it?

Money did not bring contentment to Prince Siddattha. He had a luxurious life in a palace with all of the material possessions he could want, but he still felt that something was missing in his life. He also became a holy man and nearly starved himself to death, which did not bring him the satisfaction he desired either.

The Buddha believed that the Middle Way made the path to Enlightenment easier. He taught that seeing the value in life is important, not material possessions. He taught that wealth is impermanent. It is therefore foolish to dedicate your life to it or to spend time chasing after it. It cannot bring long-term happiness.

This does not mean that Buddhists think money is not important or that it is wrong to earn it. But they think that how the money is earned is important, and they try to make sure the jobs they do qualify as Right Livelihood (see Unit 2.3).

The story opposite, from the Payasi Sutta in the Digha Nikāya, shows that giving to those in need is very important. Buddhists believe that giving creates good kamma, which benefits individuals and the whole community.

> 'Riches kill the fool, but not those who are about to go to the far shore. Because of craving for riches a fool kills himself just as [he kills] others.'
> Dhammapada 355

a The Beckhams are an example of a famous rich couple.

The Tale of Prince Payasi

During the time of the Buddha, there lived a prince named Payasi, who set up a charity for holy men, travellers, beggars and the needy. However, he gave low quality food, including broken rice and sour gruel, as well as rough clothing. Payasi put a young man named Uttara in charge of handing out the supplies to the people in need.

One day Prince Payasi heard that Uttara had been criticising him behind his back. The prince summoned him and asked, 'But why did you say such a thing? Friend Uttara, don't we who wish to gain merit expect a reward for our charity?'

Uttara replied, 'But Lord, the food you give – broken rice with sour gruel – you would not care to touch it with your foot, much less eat it! And the rough clothes – you would not care to set foot on them, much less wear them!'

Prince Payasi then asked Uttara to supply better food and clothing, and Uttara did so. When Prince Payasi died he was reborn in an empty mansion in a low heavenly realm. Uttara was reborn in a higher heavenly realm of greater comforts.

b The Tale of Prince Payasi considers the importance of charitable giving.

Reflection

Do you think that a 'wealth of excellent virtue' is more important than material wealth? Why or why not?

Activities

1 Create a poster to promote the Middle Way. Do you think it is a good way to live? Why or why not?

2 Using the teachings of the Buddha, design an emblem to remind Buddhists of his teachings on wealth and poverty, and the importance of following the Middle Way.

3 What does the story of Prince Payasi have to say about the motivation behind charitable giving? Make a list of good reasons to give to charity and a list of bad reasons.

4 Plan a script for a drama of the story above. Think about the characters you will need and where it will be set. You could set it in modern times.

Do Animals have Rights?

Learning Objectives

In this unit you will:

- explain Buddhist views on animal rights
- identify the significance of kamma in relation to this issue
- reflect on how you think animals should be treated.

The First Precept (see Unit 2.4) is to not take the life of any living creature, so many Buddhists choose to be vegetarians. They think that all of life is important, that they have no right to harm others, and that killing another creature is wrong.

Buddhists also believe in a direct link between actions and consequences. This affects the way they behave.

> 'All tremble at violence; all fear death. Comparing [others] with oneself, one should not kill or cause others to kill.'
> Dhammapada 129

Mrs Aldam is a Buddhist, but sometimes eats meat because her husband likes to eat it. She says, 'When I do eat meat, I try to make sure it is free range and produced as humanely as possible.' She and her granddaughter Molly are very much against intensive and battery farming because they think that animals should be treated with respect.

Boonyoung thinks that animal rights are very important. He says that the Buddha teaches people to respect and live in harmony with all life, so harming, killing or interfering with animals is wrong. He says, 'I think that if you give them suffering, it's not good, if you give them suffering, you receive that same suffering in your heart.'

> 'By eating meat we share the responsibility of climate change, the destruction of our forests and the poisoning of our air and water. The simple act of becoming a vegetarian will make a difference in the health of our planet.'
> Thich Nhat Hanh, *The World We Have*

? Why do you think the concept of free range farming would be important to many Buddhists?

Buddhists are realistic about their principles. It is not compulsory for Buddhists to be vegetarian and, although the Dalai Lama (see Unit 4.3) lives as a vegetarian at his home in India, he does not keep to a strict vegetarian diet when he is travelling.

Most Buddhists would agree that it is wrong to experiment on animals for cosmetic purposes. They would also find it very hard to be involved in that type of work because it is not a Right Livelihood (see Unit 2.3). Some Buddhists think that animal experimentation for medical research can be allowed because it reduces more suffering than it creates.

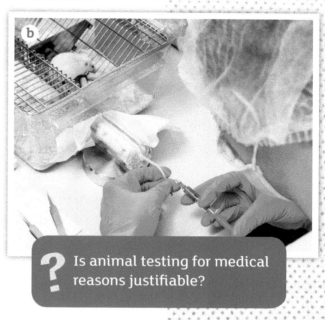

? Is animal testing for medical reasons justifiable?

Molly disagrees with animal testing, especially when it is for non-essential reasons like cosmetics. She says, 'I think it is really wrong for humans to take advantage of animals just because we are more intelligent than them, because they suffer just the same as us.'

Activities

1. Explain why it is important for Buddhists to respect all of life.
2. 'Human life is more important than animal life.' Decide where you stand and prepare your arguments for a class debate on this statement.
3. Plan a year group assembly on the theme of animal rights, using the information in this unit.

Reflection

'Be kind to all that lives.' Is this good guidance?

Learning Objectives

In this unit you will:

- develop further understanding of Buddhist teaching on conflict
- explain different views on the use of violence and non-violence
- reflect on the place of non-violence in the modern world.

Starter

- Can you imagine a world without any violence? What would it be like?

Mahayana Buddhism teaches that all people have the 'Buddha-nature' within them, meaning that everyone has the potential for Enlightenment. Therefore, Buddhists seek to respect and protect the dignity and rights of each person.

Buddhist teaching also makes it very clear that violence is not acceptable – after all, the First Precept is to avoid taking life. Through the Noble Eightfold Path, Buddhists learn not to harm people or things by practising Right Action. This means they would try to avoid taking any job that meant using force or violence.

a The Buddha taught about non-violence through the Noble Eightfold Path.

Case Study

Tom says, 'I don't find the Buddhist teachings about non-violence difficult to follow because I have never really been in a situation where I had to use violence. If I had been or if somebody else threatened me, I would just talk my way out of it. If everybody in the world had the same view as me on non-violence, the world would be better. But for [...] everybody to achieve that would be next to impossible.'

But there are times when Buddhism is associated with violence. Martial arts have strong links with Buddhist philosophy and spirituality, and are focused on self-control rather than doing harm. In Buddhist forms of martial arts, there are very strict rules about how violence can be used. Monks and nuns are allowed to defend themselves, but they are forbidden to kill, even in self-defence.

There are examples of Buddhist involvement in violence. During the 1960s, some Buddhist monks protested about the American war in Vietnam by setting themselves on fire. More recently, some Tibetan Buddhists took their lives in the same way as a protest against the Chinese government's occupation of Tibet.

However, many more Buddhists take a non-violent approach to promote peace and justice. The Japanese Buddhist monk Nichidatsu Fujii founded the Nipponzan-Myohoji order, which is part of the school of Pure Land Buddhism (see Unit 3.5). He dedicated his life to spreading the message of non-violence, and his order organizes peace pilgrimages and builds peace pagodas around the world.

b These Shaolin monks are performing at a martial arts demonstration in China.

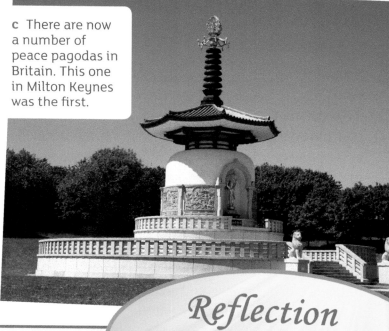

c There are now a number of peace pagodas in Britain. This one in Milton Keynes was the first.

Reflection

'One should neither kill nor cause others to kill.' How does this apply to ordinary people?

Activities

1 Can a religion promote peace and martial arts at the same time? Do you think they are compatible?

2 Tom says the world would be a better place if everyone followed the Buddhist teaching of non-violence, but that this would be next to impossible. Do you agree? Design a poster, based on Buddhist principles, that informs people about non-violence.

3 The principle of non-violence is not just important to Buddhists. Find out about other individuals or groups who have promoted non-violence. Create a presentation to show to your class.

Learning Objectives

In this unit you will:

- investigate Thich Nhat Hanh's work in promoting peace
- identify why Buddhists work for positive changes in the world
- reflect on what motivates people to help others.

Starter

- What do you think peace is?
- What do you think the phrase 'social action' means?

Thich Nhat Hanh was born in 1926 and is now a Vietnamese Buddhist master. He is also a poet and an activist for peace and human rights. Thay, as he is known to his followers, works to show how Buddhism can be used as a practical force for good and peace in the world. To do this, he founded a movement called Engaged Buddhism.

Thay works with the Plum Village monastic community in the south of France to teach people about the importance of peace, both on an individual level and on a global scale. He organizes a number of retreats and events around the world to help people from different jobs and lifestyles find more peace and fulfillment in their everyday activities.

Thay became a Buddhist monk in his home country of Vietnam at the age of 16. When war broke out between Vietnam and the USA, Thay taught people that peaceful discussion and reconciliation was the best way to avoid conflict. He left Vietnam to study and teach in the USA, but he was not allowed back into his own country for a long time.

Thay's Engaged Buddhism is a very socially aware and active form of the faith. In 1964, he founded the School of Youth for Social Service in Vietnam. This group was made up of young people and university professors and students, and provided practical relief for those affected by conflict.

'It is my conviction that there is no way to peace – peace is the way.'
Thich Nhat Hanh, *The Act of Power*

? What does Thich Nhat Hanh mean here?

b Thich Nhat Hanh organized a peace rally in Trafalgar Square, London.

Together they practised Engaged Buddhism and went around Vietnam helping people in a very practical way. This took many forms, including building health clinics and helping to repair houses that had been damaged during the Vietnam War.

Thay has been nominated for the Nobel Peace Prize and has also led many peace rallies. He led the Buddhist delegation at the Paris Peace Conference in 1973, which tried to establish peace in Vietnam. He believed that his country needed to keep to Buddhist principles for peace to really work.

This gentle monk is a well-respected figure. His teachings blend together many forms of Buddhism, from Zen and other Mahayana traditions to those from Theravada Buddhism, but his teachings also appeal to those who do not have a faith, as well as to a wide range of people from all religions. It is clear that, through his peace rallies and talks, his active form of Buddhism has had a profound impact on the western world, as well as in Vietnam.

c This peace walk took place in Los Angeles in 2007.

Reflection

Many faiths teach that helping others is very important.
Do you think that a person of faith has more motivation to help people who are in need?
Why or why not?

Activities

1. What is social action? Do you think it is important to engage in it? Do you think the world would be a better place if more people engaged in it?

2. 📄 Your school has been asked by a group that practises Engaged Buddhism to design a project that would help your local community. Identify who or what in your community needs help and think of a practical way to help them. Develop the project proposal.

3. Prepare a presentation to give to your class on the life and work of Thich Nhat Hanh. Use your own research as well as the information in this unit.

Objectives

- Identify key aspects of the Buddhist way of life
- Evaluate the importance of retreats within Buddhism
- Show understanding of Buddhism in practice by planning a retreat for lay Buddhists

Task

Plan a weekend series of workshops for British lay Buddhists. Participants will want to learn how to live out their Buddhism in a practical way and meet the challenges of life in modern Britain. They will need clear teaching on issues such as relationships, animal rights, how to deal with conflict and how to use their money.

a Plan the main elements of the programme for the workshops, which will be held in the local town hall. Participants will arrive on Friday night after work and leave on Sunday afternoon.

b Prepare a leaflet to advertise the weekend to British Buddhists.

A bit of guidance...

Aim to include Buddhist teaching and practical advice from a Buddhist perspective for lay people. Make sure that you know what Buddhists believe about the issues that you are going to focus on.

Hints and tips

To help you tackle this task, you could:

- research what happens on Buddhist retreats
- focus on three or four specific issues
- explain your ideas in a clear and interesting way.

Guidance

What level are you aiming at? Have a look at the grid below to see what you need to do to achieve that level. What would you need to do to improve your work?

	I can...
Level 3	• use some religious vocabulary and sources to show my understanding of some Buddhist beliefs and teachings • explain what a lay person is and why learning more about Buddhism could be important to a lay Buddhist • express my own views on the value of taking time out for reflection.
Level 4	• use religious vocabulary and sources to describe and explain some Buddhist beliefs and teachings on ethical issues • identify how learning more about Buddhism could help a lay person to cope with modern life • express my own ideas on the value of taking time out for reflection.
Level 5	• use a wide range of religious vocabulary and sources to describe and explain Buddhist beliefs on a variety of ethical issues relevant today • analyse and explain how learning more about Buddhism might help people to live authentically as Buddhists in Britain • express well-informed opinions about the value of taking time out for reflection, linking my ideas to Buddhist teachings.
Level 6	• use religious vocabulary and sources to critically evaluate and discuss Buddhist beliefs on a variety of ethical issues relevant today • analyse and explain the impact of learning more about Buddhism on helping people to live authentically as Buddhists in Britain • evaluate my own and others' perspectives on the value of taking time out for reflection, drawing on my learning about Buddhist teachings.

Ready for more?

When you have completed this task, you can also work on your skills for Levels 6 and 7, and perhaps even higher. This is an extension task.

You could now go on to fill in the more detailed aspects of your programme for the workshops. Think about who you might ask to talk, as well as what worship and leisure activities will take place.

Glossary

Abhidhamma basket The deeper, philosophical teachings of the Buddha

Anatta The Buddhist belief that there is no permanent self or 'soul'

Anicca Impermanence in the world; everything changes and nothing lasts forever

Anjali mudda The gesture of putting the hands together in a prayer-like position and bowing the head

Ascetic Someone who lives a life of self-denial, often in order to reach a spiritual goal

BCE Stands for 'before the Common Era', which began roughly 2000 years ago

Bhavacakka Buddhist art that represents the universe symbolically

Bhikkhu Buddhist monk

Bhikkhuni Buddhist nun

Bodhi tree A type of fig tree

Bodhisattva Wise Buddhists who keep coming back to the world after they die to help others

Buddha The Enlightened One; a person who discovers Enlightenment for themself

Buddharupa An image of the Buddha

Canon A collection of sacred writings

CE Stands for 'Common Era', which began roughly 2000 years ago

Craving A constant desire for things and experiences

Dalai Lama The spiritual and political leader of Tibetan Buddhism

Dhamma The teachings of the Buddha

Dhamma Wheel (Dhammacakka) A wheel with eight spokes that is a symbol of Buddhism and represents the Noble Eightfold Path

Dukkha Dissatisfaction or suffering in life

Enlightenment The state of full understanding about the way things are in life

Ethical Living and working by doing the 'right' thing

Five Precepts Practical, ethical guidelines for living a Buddhist life

Four Noble Truths The Buddha's teachings on the nature of suffering: illness, cause, cure exists, cure

Four Sights The four sights that deeply affected Siddattha: an old man, a sick man, a dead body and a holy man

GDP Gross Domestic Product; the total value of all goods and services produced by an economy

GNH Gross National Happiness

Impermanence When something doesn't last and can change

Kamma/karma Actions that are the result of the choices people make

Koan A puzzle-like question that a Zen master asks a novice or trainee

Lama A Tibetan Buddhist teacher or leader

Lay People who follow a faith but are not ordained

Lotus flower A flower that is similar to a water lily and is a symbol of Buddhism

Mahayana The Great Vehicle; one of two main schools of Buddhism

Mandala A sacred design within a circle

Mantra Words to meditate on and focus the mind

Middle Way A life that involves neither great excess and extravagance nor great poverty and deprivation

Multicultural A society that contains several different cultural groups

Multifaith Something that involves a variety of faiths

Neuroscience Studies that focus on the structure and function of the brain and nervous system

Nibbana/Nirvana 'Blowing out' the fires of greed, hatred and ignorance, and the state of perfect peace that follows

Nibbana Day/Nirvana Day Celebrates the Buddha's death and his reaching a final Nibbana; occurs in February

Nipponzan-Myohoji A school of Mahayana Buddhism that developed in Japan

Noble Eightfold Path The Buddha's Middle Way: Right Understanding, Right Attitude, Right Speech, Right Action, Right Livelihood, Right Effort, Right Mindfulness, Right Contemplation

Ordained Those who, in Buddhism, train to be and are made into monks and nuns

Pali The language of many early Buddhist scriptures; an ancient language originating in northern India

PhD A high-level academic qualification

Prostration A movement where the body is laid flat on the ground, with the face down, before getting up again

Puja Buddhist worship

Pure Land School of Buddhism that believes in reaching Enlightenment through meditation on Amida Buddha

Retreat A withdrawal from everyday life for a period of quiet thoughtfulness, usually in a monastery

Samana A holy man who lives a life of poverty

Samsara The endless cycle of birth, death and rebirth, with all its suffering

Sangha The community of Buddhist believers

Sanskrit The ancient sacred language of India

Secular Without religious reference; non-religious

Siddattha or Siddhartha The personal name of the Buddha

Stupa A conical object that represents the Buddha's holy mind

Sutta/sutra Text; the word of the Buddha

Sutta basket The most well-known teachings of the Buddha

Theist A person who believes in the existence of a god or gods

Theravada The Way of the Elders; one of two main schools of Buddhism

Three Refuges/Three Jewels The three most precious things in Buddhism: the Buddha, the dhamma, the Sangha

Three Signs of Being Anicca, dukkha, anatta

Tibetan Buddhism A school of Mahayana Buddhism that developed in Tibet

Tipitaka The Three Baskets; the three collections of writings that make up the Pali Canon

Upsaka A member of the lay Buddhist community

Vinaya basket The teachings of the Buddha that make up the set of rules for monastic life

Wesak A festival on the full moon of the month Wesak (in May or June) to celebrate the birth, Enlightenment and death of the Buddha

Zazen Seated meditation

Zen Buddhism 'Zen' comes from the Sanskrit word meaning 'meditation' or 'concentration'; a school of Mahayana Buddhism that developed in China and Japan

Index